Adobe Photoshop Elements 2025 Guidebook

A Comprehensive Manual for Creative Enhancements and Seamless Photo Editing from Beginners to Experts

Tim Elvis

CHAPTER ONE
ADOBE PHOTOSHOP ELEMENTS 2025
INTRODUCTION

A Synopsis of Photoshop Elements

The purpose of Adobe Photoshop Elements is to make picture editing simple and comprehensive for both casual users and photo experts. Because it combines sophisticated features with simplicity of use, this program is often chosen by those who want to edit images but don't want to learn how to use Adobe Photoshop. People of all skill levels may use Photoshop Elements because of its user-friendly interface. Additionally, it offers several capabilities for organizing, sharing, and enhancing images. One of the most crucial components of Photoshop Elements is the interface. The three primary editing modes are Advanced, Guided, and Quick. Each option offers varying degrees of control over the editing process. Simple Mode is intended for users who want to make simple alterations, including correcting lighting or contrast, while Guided Mode provides step-by-step assistance for more specialized edits, like retouching portraits or creating picture collages. Despite being more sophisticated, Advanced Mode is still simpler to use than Photoshop's complete version. For those who want to learn more about editing techniques like layer work and sophisticated retouching, it offers manual tools. Adobe Sensei makes extensive use of artificial intelligence (AI) to operate many of the software's automated capabilities. For instance, Photoshop Elements makes it simple to colorize black-and-white images, eliminate extraneous items, or let the application choose topics in a picture automatically. These AI-powered capabilities speed up and simplify editing so even novice users can do complex operations like altering the backdrop or eliminating items. Photoshop Elements also allows you to be creative with its many effects and filters. With a few clicks, images may be given a distinctive appearance, such as an artistic finish or a vintage appearance. Additionally, users may use motion effects to include dynamic elements into their images, including moving backdrops or twinkling stars. This adds a dynamic touch to personal projects and social media postings.

The Elements Organizer program offers you strong organizing capabilities in addition to picture editing. By enabling users to categorize, organize, and even search for photographs using geotagging, face recognition, and other information, this program aids users in managing their expanding photo collections. Whether you are keeping a variety of family photographs or holiday photos, the Organizer helps you keep everything organized and accessible. Photoshop Elements has the advantage of not requiring a subscription, unlike Adobe Creative Cloud. For those who don't want to pay fees again, the fact that it may be purchased just once is advantageous. For those on a tight budget who wants high-quality editing tools but is unable to commit to a long-term plan, this makes it an excellent option. The latest versions of Adobe, including the 2025 release, provide new motion effects; enhanced depth control with AI-powered blur filters, compatibility for the Apple M3 CPU for quicker performance, and even more guided edits to help users improve. With over 50 suggested adjustments, users may always learn something new while making improvements to their images. Photoshop Elements is a full-featured picture editing application. It may be used for everything from simple adjustments and organization to fine-tuning and more complicated undertakings. All users can get the most out of their images thanks to the combination of sophisticated AI-powered tools and user-friendly features, eliminating the need to spend time learning how to use expensive software.

2025 Adobe Photoshop Elements

The most recent iteration of the well-known Photoshop substitute, Adobe Photoshop Elements 2025, is geared more at novices and amateurs and requires no subscription; instead, a one-time licensing cost with a fixed three-year period is required. It is available alone or in combination with Adobe Premiere Elements, which is a user-friendly version of Adobe Premiere Pro that is equally suitable for novices. Considering how inexpensive it is, Photoshop Elements 2025 ought to be regarded as one of the greatest photo editing applications. Within this small group, there is additional software called the Elements 2025 Organizer. This little cataloging application is helpful. It functions as a central location for Photoshop and Premiere elements and provides search tools and albums.

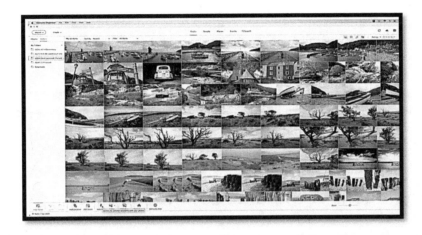

What's new in Adobe Photoshop Elements 2025?

Photoshop Elements 2025 has a ton of new features that may convince you to upgrade from an earlier version. Even if there is no change, you should look more closely at the new features. They include simpler enhancements and jazzy effects. For example, Elements 2025 now offers AI object removal, which allows you to paint over any unwanted item and use data from the surrounding image to make it seem to be absent. The new Guided Edit is now available to assist you with the process.

Elements 2025 also has the depth of field blur that was first introduced in Lightroom. Again, AI is used to detach individuals from their contexts, and it does so rather well. This filter is in the Advanced mode, which is confusing. Depth of Field Guided Edit is one that seems like it ought to be but isn't. This one employs a fairly simple topic selection technique or a tilt-shift effect. Although the automated selection tools allow you to alter the color of any item, the old-fashioned selection tools are difficult to use and the blending isn't always seamless. This would function much more effectively with the AI topic selection features seen in other apps. I'm meant to be able to "seamlessly" combine different backgrounds, objects, and other components, even though this seems to only stack them in layers and provide you with basic foreground and background object selection features. Four new Quick Actions have been added. One of them enables you to add motion to static images in a manner reminiscent of a movie trailer. This is very nice, however you have to export it to see how it appears since there isn't a preview option. Adobe has also released a mobile app and online companion to go along with Elements 2025; however both are currently in beta testing. Even though Elements 2025 has a lot of new features, it is still based on an outdated interface and process.

A brief synopsis of the characteristics

- **Brush for Object Removal:** Both the Removal Brush and the Object Removal Brush use AI technology from Adobe Firefly. They function similarly to the Generative Fill tool in Photoshop. The main difference is that the tool uses information from your photo to fill in the spaces; there is no text to replace what you remove. The most of the time it works, but sometimes it doesn't. All things considered, it's a helpful tool for quickly removing objects or background people.

- **Blur Filter with Depth:** The Depth Blur effect is a fun way to add aperture depth to your post-production image. When shooting a photo, it's better to use a narrow depth of field, but sometimes you don't even consider it. AI allows you to blur the remainder of the picture while keeping a portion of it crisp. It does not employ depth perception to choose a region of the flat image; instead, you may select a point within a certain distance of the camera. Compared to the iPhone Portrait lens, this filter is fantastic since it gives the image a more realistic appearance.

+ **The Fast Recolor Tool:** The Quick Recolor tool in the 2025 update is my favorite feature. You may locate it in the Advanced tools by choosing Smart Brushes and choosing a preset from the thumbnails. It functions similarly to Photoshop's Quick Selection tool, except the selection's color is altered by your preset as it appears. Although the success rate varies, you may get realistic recolored effects if your image has significant color variations and you experiment with the mix modes after selection.

The Tool for Combining Photos: You can find the new "Combine Photos" function under "Guided tools." It's a simple tool for creating collages out of images. This tool may be used in a variety of ways. It has the ability to eliminate topics from backgrounds or backgrounds from subjects. Additionally, it may make two images seem to be one by combining their colors. Combining your photos allows you to experiment with a wide range of effects. The tools represented by the Guided edits have built-in guides. You may use the tool on your photographs and follow the instructions if you choose a guided edit.

Motion Graphics New: Photoshop Elements contains animated visuals with music, despite being a picture editing application.

The update included four new animated graphics:

- Sparkles Overlay
- Blinking Heart Graphic
- Pink Frame
- Zoom In-Out

These motion graphics add a little something more to your photographs with easy-to-use editing tools. My favorite tool is Zoom In-Out. The water seems to be flowing when I utilize it in a waterscape photograph.

- **Mobile and Web Apps:** Beta versions of the web and mobile applications are available with the 2025 release. Anyone using Photoshop Elements may utilize these beta versions. The first is Photoshop Elements on the Web, which functions similarly to Adobe Express or Photoshop on the Web and is accessible via your browser. As long as you can log in and connect to the internet, you can utilize the tool when you're not at home. The second is the smartphone app in beta. It is comparable to the mobile version of Photoshop Express Premium. As of this writing, users may only get it from Adobe via TestFlight. One excellent feature of the program is its offline editing capability. It excites me to see this become a real application. Adobe Photoshop Elements is a fantastic option if you want to utilize Adobe's editing tools but don't want to shell out hundreds of dollars for them. Although Photoshop Elements lacks Photoshop's flexibility and capability, it does include several fascinating capabilities that can make remarkable changes to your photos.

2025 Adobe Photoshop Elements: Cost and accessibility

Adobe Photoshop Elements 2025 is now available for $99.99, £86.99, or AU$145.99 on the Adobe website. Also available for $149.99, £130.49, or AU$219.99 are Adobe Photoshop Elements 2025 and Premiere Elements 2025 together. But bear in mind that according to Adobe's licensing agreement, "Photoshop Elements 2025 is now sold as a full 3-year term license with no monthly or annual recurring subscription." As a result, it's neither a subscription nor a perpetual license. The tail is harmed by that.

System prerequisites and interoperability

Regarding Windows

- **Operating System:** Microsoft Windows 11 (only 64-bit versions) and Windows 10 version 21H1 or later are compatible. Windows 7 and 8 are no longer usable.
- **CPU:** A minimum of an AMD CPU compatible with SSE4.1 or an Intel 6th generation processor. You should get an Intel Core i7 CPU or above for increased performance.
- **Memory (RAM):** Adobe recommends 16 GB for optimal performance, particularly when working with large files or multitasking. However, you need have at least 8 GB of RAM.
- **Hard disk Space:** To install, your hard disk must have at least 8 GB of free space; more space will be needed as the installation progresses. For more seamless operations, a solid-state drive (SSD) is preferable.
- **Graphics:** A graphics card compatible with DirectX 12 is required. The program works best with a GPU that is dedicated to that job when applying effects like depth blur or several layers.
- **Display:** For optimal editing, Adobe recommends a higher resolution, like as 1920x1080, but you must have a display with at least 1280x800 pixels.
- **Internet connection:** necessary for online service access, subscription validation, and product activation.

Regarding macOS

- **Minimum operating system:** macOS 12.0 (Monterey). Older models, such as Big Sur or Catalina, will not function in the 2025 version.
- **CPU:** A 64-bit multicore Intel CPU or an Apple Silicon (M1/M2/M3) processor for more recent Macs. Improved speed and energy efficiency are the results of full support for the Apple M3 processor.
- **Memory (RAM):** It is recommended to have at least 8 GB, but 16 GB is preferable for editing huge files or doing extensive work on them.
- **Hard Drive Space:** To install, you'll need 8 GB of free space, plus additional space for project files and media, just as with Windows.
- **Graphics:** A GPU compatible with Metal is required. Using a dedicated graphics card improves the software's performance for more complex tasks.

- **Display:** Higher resolutions are recommended for better editing, although a minimum of 1280x800 is needed.
- **Internet:** To activate and use internet tools, you must have it.

Considerations for Compatibility

- **File Format Support:** Photoshop Elements 2025 is compatible with a wide range of picture files, including RAW, TIFF, PNG, and JPEG from many camera manufacturers. MP4 and MOV are supported for video, particularly when Premiere Elements is utilized.
- **Apple Silicon Compatibility:** Users of the most recent Mac models should anticipate improved performance thanks to full support for Apple M1, M2, and M3 chipsets, particularly when using resource-intensive functions like AI object removal and picture compositing.
- **Peripherals:** The program is compatible with common peripherals, such as Wacom tablets, which are helpful for accurate image editing. As long as printers and scanners are compatible with your operating system, you may use them.
- **Integration with Creative Cloud:** Photoshop Elements may be used with other Adobe products if necessary, but it is not a part of Creative Cloud. Adobe Photoshop Elements Organizer, which enables users to arrange and transfer their media assets across devices, makes it compatible with mobile applications.

For optimal performance, it is preferable to go above and above the bare minimal requirements whenever possible, particularly when working on intricate edits or high-resolution photos. Your computer will function more smoothly if it has a dedicated GPU, more RAM, and a quicker CPU. This is particularly true when using AI-powered features like Depth Blur and Subject Selection.

CHAPTER TWO

ABOUT SETUP, ACTIVATION, AND INSTALLATION

Adobe Photoshop Elements 2025 is simple to set up and install, but you must take care to ensure a flawless experience. Whether you're upgrading from an earlier version or downloading the application for the first time, follow these steps to ensure a seamless download.

Prior to starting

+ Verify that you have administrator permissions to the account you are using.
+ Verify that you are using the most current version of Chrome, Firefox, Safari, or Internet Explorer.
+ Verify the validity of your Adobe ID.
+ Disable any browser extensions that prevent pop-ups.
+ For a brief while, turn off firewalls, antivirus programs, and third-party security software. Turning them off expedites the installation procedure.
+ Prior to the installation being completed, confirm that you have Internet connectivity.

Getting the Software

+ **Purchase or Access via Adobe:** Photoshop Elements 2025 is available on the Adobe website (https://www.adobe.com/products/photoshop-elements/free-trial.html) or through a licensed reseller. Because Adobe offers older customers a discount when they upgrade, be sure to have your account details handy if you're upgrading. You'll need to create an Adobe account if you don't already have one.
+ **Download from Adobe Website:** After purchasing the program, locate the Photoshop Elements section on Adobe's website. A download link for the Windows and macOS versions may be found there. Select the link that corresponds to your operating system.

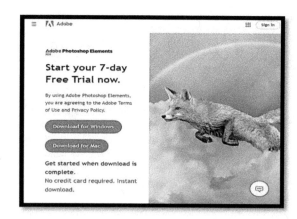

- **Download Adobe Creative Cloud (Optional):** Photoshop Elements does not need Creative Cloud, but if you use other Adobe applications, downloading the Adobe Creative Cloud app makes managing updates and installations simpler.

Detailed Installation Instructions

- **Find the Installer:** After downloading the file, locate the installer in your Downloads folder. PhotoshopElements_2025_Mac.dmg for macOS or PhotoshopElements_2025_Win.exe for Windows are the correct names for it.
- **launch the installer:**
  - ➢ **Windows:** Double-clicking the.exe file will launch the installation procedure. You could be prompted by User Account Control to consent to system modifications. If so, choose "Yes."
  - ➢ **macOS:** After mounting the.dmg file with a double-click, Mac users should drag the Photoshop Elements 2025 icon into the Applications folder.
- **Comply with the Installation Guide:**
  - ➢ The installation procedure will be guided by the setup wizard. To install the software, you will be prompted to choose a location. It's better to place it in the default location (the Applications folder for macOS or the C: Drive for Windows) unless you have a compelling reason to do otherwise.

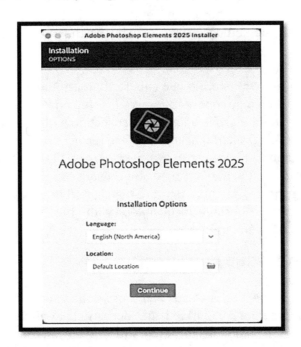

  - ➢ You may be prompted to add other files during the installation process, including Microsoft Visual C++ Redistributable (for Windows users), which are necessary for the program to function correctly.

11

- **Language and Preferences:** After the installation begins, you will be prompted to choose your preferred language and choose a few installation parameters, such as whether to execute the application after it has completed or create desktop shortcuts.
- **Installation Completion:** After the installation is complete, click Finish. If you want to have Photoshop Elements 2025 launch automatically, it will launch for the first time.

Primary Configuration and Setup

- **First-Time Launch:** Photoshop Elements may take a few minutes to set up and prepare for usage on your computer when you first launch it. During this time, it will look for updates. When the program first launches, the Welcome Screen will appear. This panel allows you to make guided modifications, browse tutorials, and begin a new project.
- **Sign in with Adobe ID:** Before you can use the software, you must sign in using the same Adobe ID account that you used to purchase or register it. Adobe will prompt you to create one if you don't already have one when you first set it up.
- **Activation:** After logging in, the program will launch automatically if you purchased it from Adobe's website. The product serial number, which may be found on the box or in the email confirming your purchase, must be provided if you have a retail or boxed copy. Follow the instructions on the screen to complete activation.
- **Customizing Preferences:** Select Edit > Preferences (Windows) or Photoshop Elements > Preferences (macOS) once Photoshop Elements has been enabled. In the options menu, you may adjust basic settings (such how bright the user interface should be), file processing, and performance parameters (like how much RAM the program should utilize).
- **Configure Organizer (Optional):** If you choose to utilize the Elements Organizer, now is the time to do so. You may choose to forego this step and import your films and images at a later time. You can manage your media collection with the aid of AI capabilities like event-based organizing, smart labeling, and face recognition.
- **Guided Tour:** Adobe provides a useful overview of Photoshop Elements when you launch the application for the first time. The Advanced mode, Quick Edits, and Guided Edits are among the key features that are highlighted in this tour of the UI. This is an excellent method to become acquainted with the program's appearance and functionality if you haven't used it before.

Solving Activation Issues

Make sure your internet connection is steady and that Adobe's servers aren't being blocked by your firewall or antivirus program if you have issues during activation. If your activation limit has been surpassed, you may also disable the program on additional devices. To manage your devices, visit the Adobe website and sign in with your credentials.

Final Notes on Setup

It's recommended to maintain your application updated once it has been configured and enabled. You may check for updates in Photoshop Elements by using the Help menu. Regular software updates provide you with the most recent features, security patches, and bug fixes. You may also sync your work across devices running Adobe Elements Organizer by using the mobile app. After the installation is complete, you may begin creating artistic things using Photoshop Elements, such as picture editing and sophisticated compositing.

CHAPTER THREE
PHOTOSHOP ELEMENTS 2025: STARTING OFF
Comprehending the Workplace

The straightforward, tidy workspace of Photoshop Elements is suitable for users of all experience levels, from total novices to seasoned enthusiasts. This section's several sections are designed to facilitate editing and provide you with instant access to the tools you need whenever you need them.

About Home Screen

When you initially launch Photoshop Elements 2025, you begin on the Home Screen. This core hub provides access to several tasks and projects, making it simple to begin editing immediately or pick up new abilities. The layout is designed to be simple enough that even newcomers may navigate it without getting lost.

Primary Carousel

At the top of the Home Screen is a Main Carousel that displays various highlights, such as tips, seasonal material, and new features. The purpose of this section is to inform users about the most recent Adobe releases. To help users rapidly grasp how to utilize new capabilities, such as AI Object Removal or Depth Blur, the carousel will showcase them with brief explanations or videos. It also offers seasonal advice, such as how to create effects that are appropriate for certain occasions or edit photos with holiday themes. This section ensures that consumers may use the most recent tools and are aware of them.

Editors of Pictures and Videos

Directly under the Main Carousel is the section designated for Photo and Video Editors. It has buttons that make opening the workspaces for editing photos and videos simple. If you have both Photoshop Elements and Premiere Elements loaded, you will see both options. You may start editing photographs in Quick, Guided, or Advanced modes as soon as you click the Photo Editor Button, which will transport you to the center of Photoshop Elements. You may work on your video projects in Premiere Elements by clicking the Video Editor Button for the same purpose. Because users can begin editing immediately without having to go through additional menus, this structure facilitates work.

Automatic Creations

One of the greatest features in Photoshop Elements 2025 is Auto Creations, which appears as a section on the Home Screen. This functionality is powered by Adobe Sensei, the company's AI technology. It automatically creates artistic projects like collages, slideshows, and animations using the images and videos you input. Depending on the material you have, Auto Creations may choose to create a presentation using your holiday photographs or an entertaining collage using images from a recent occasion. A sneak peek of these pieces is available on the Home Screen. You may alter things to make them even better if you like what you see. This eliminates the need to start from scratch and makes it incredibly easy to create material that appears polished and professional.

Elements Guided Edits

Photoshop Elements' Guided Edits tool is fantastic, and it's simple to access from the Home Screen. Users may do certain tasks, such as removing items from a photo, creating a double exposure effect, or altering the lighting in a portrait, step-by-step using Guided Edits. For those who are new to editing, this tool is ideal since it builds on their existing knowledge and teaches them new abilities. Users may begin the lessons immediately since the Home Screen displays some of the most well-liked and often used Guided Edits. With every new update, Adobe continues to introduce additional Guided Edits, giving customers a variety to choose from.

Recent Projects

"Recent Projects" is a helpful feature that displays thumbnails of your most recent photo or video editing projects. With this function, you don't have to travel through folders one by one to get to the stuff you've been working on. Clicking on any of the thumbnails will instantly open the project in the relevant edit, whether it's a picture or a video. By making it simple to locate your most recent work, this section keeps your workflow efficient. You won't have to wait to continue editing where you left off.

Inspiration Feed

The Inspiration Feed on the Home Screen provides users with a constant flow of original ideas and instructional videos. Adobe constantly updates this feed with project ideas, advice from professional artists, and even challenges designed to encourage experimentation. Whether you're searching for Christmas card ideas, improved photo editing techniques, or ways to add motion to a photo, this feed has it all. Users may watch videos that demonstrate how to achieve certain effects or click on links to get in-depth instructions. There is always something fresh to learn and something to be inspired by for anybody looking to become better at editing.

Help Resources

The Help Resources section has direct connections to various forms of assistance. These consist of customer support, forums, and manuals. Adobe included a link to their extensive collection of videos and documentation on the Home Screen because they understand that customers may sometimes run into issues or want assistance. User manuals, problem-solving books, and video tutorials covering everything from basic tasks to more complex issues are available. Links to forums where other users of Photoshop Elements may discuss their experiences or pose queries are also provided. With customer support only a click away; consumers can access expert assistance for more significant issues when they need it.

Advanced, Guided, and Fast Modes

A Quick Edit

In Photo Editor, a distinct application from Organizer, Adobe's editing capabilities are divided across three displays, or edit modes. I recommend starting with the Quick Edit mode if you've never used Elements before. This is the most straightforward method of alteration. The "before" view, "after" view, or any other view style may be selected by users who are modifying an image in Quick Edit mode. Some of the amazing effects that you may employ with a single click are shown on the right side of Quick Edit mode. Click the Effects tab to access them. There are several options available to you. You just need to click once to see results with this fantastic tool, and many of them are moving. To edit the photos, you will use the Organizer to find and choose them. Depending on your needs, they will then open in one or more of the three editing modes. When you're done editing them, they are saved and show up in the Organizer as fresh. Keep in mind that you may switch between the three editing techniques. If necessary, it is simple to switch an image between Quick, Guided, and Advanced. The Quick Edit tool allows users to make little but significant adjustments to any image by using various color modifications. To make changing them faster, this is arranged in a certain order, from most essential to least important. Smart Fix, Exposure, Lighting, Color, and Sharpness are some of the settings that may be changed. **Among the tools available in this mode are the following:**

- **Hand tool:** This allows you to manipulate large pictures on the screen.
- **Quick Selection Tool:** Perfect for selectively picking out and highlighting certain regions of an image.
- **Zoom tool:** This tool allows you to adjust the size of objects on the screen.
- **Eye tool:** Made to eliminate green and red pet eyes.
- **Whiten Teeth tool:** Selects teeth and uses a single click to make them whiter.
- **Straighten tool:** Levels out uneven distances.
- **Type tool:** intended to add text to an image without any spaces between words.
- **Spot Healing and Healing Brush tools:** These are effective methods for repairing and enhancing images.
- **Crop tool:** To allow for frame recomposition, the crop tool is often used to eliminate portions of an image.
- **Move tool:** This tool is excellent for rearranging text and other picture components.

You may modify the way each tool functions in all editing modes by clicking to bring up the Tool Options panel at the bottom of the screen.

About Guided Edit

The Guided Edit workspace has detailed instructions. From simple activities like adjusting tones to far more complex ones like creating panoramas and adding unique type effects, these tips will assist you with a broad variety of jobs. All 47 of them are easy to use and have a nice appearance. Select an effect, and then just follow the easy instructions. Basics, Color, Black & White, Fun Edits, Special Edits, and Photomerge—a little tool that can, among other things, combine images to create widescreen panoramas—are covered. Guided Edit mode lets you be creative. When you choose the Basics tab, the Guided Edit screen looks like this. Although there is a lot going on on this screen, it is easy to comprehend what each effect does to the samples since it is always changing. This feature, in my opinion, is much underappreciated.

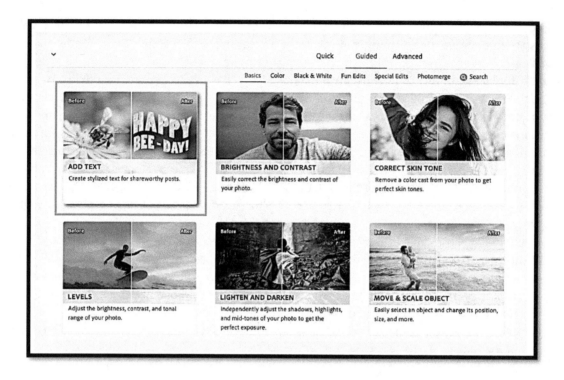

You may slide the mouse pointer left or right over each thumbnail to see a "before" and "after" photo. These are excellent suggestions for creating software that may be used in a wide range of applications. Some individuals believe that the Guided Edit mode is more imaginative than my current Home screen. For example, open a photograph in this mode and experiment with some of the effects if you're unsure about how to edit your photos. The majority of these will inspire you to come up with something original. This mode serves as an intuitive manual that demonstrates a simplified method for achieving certain outcomes for both novice and expert users. Creating visually beautiful and shareable material is now a simple and enjoyable process thanks to Photoshop Elements 2025's new Add Text tool and user-friendly UI.

Advanced Editing

For those who are new to picture editing, switching to the Advanced Editing workspace after experimenting with the Quick Edit and Guided Edit modes may seem challenging. However, it might be useful to enter the Advanced Edit mode with a clear editing strategy, or a general notion of how you want the image to appear. It helps to be somewhat acquainted with the tools in order to utilize the Advanced Edit mode effectively. Although the Advanced Edit mode is comparable to Adobe Photoshop, it includes many special operations that Photoshop does not. Your expertise with the first two edit modes will provide you a starting point.

Despite its intimidating name, the Advanced Edit mode's core tools are quite simple to use and provide a wide range of creative possibilities. Compared to the Quick and Guided Edit modes, this option allows you to make more changes. Although mastering the tools requires practice and effort, having experimented with them in the novice levels might facilitate the transition to the advanced realm. In this mode, the main window has a Photo Bin in the lower left corner for navigating between open images files, along with controls for Rotate, Undo, and Redo. Fine-tuning tool performance is possible via the current tool's Options panel, which gives you exact control over each tool's efficacy and, therefore, the editing outcomes. When your photos are really amazing, you should post them on social media, print them, or use them in a project like a photo book or movie. The Create and Share options are quite useful in this situation since they make these tasks simple.

Overview of Panels and Toolbars

The Panel Bin

The Panel Bin is a crucial component of the workspace in Adobe Photoshop Elements that facilitates access to various tools and settings. It is located on the right side of the screen and allows users to control effects, layers, and other elements in both Quick and Advanced editing modes. Because it maintains the primary workspace free while enabling users to rapidly access changes and capabilities, the Panel Bin is a crucial component of keeping users organized while they work on their projects.

Important Elements of the Panel Bin

- **Layers Panel:** Especially in Advanced Mode, the Layers panel is one of the most important components in the Panel Bin. It enables users to manage the various project layers. Layers are a crucial component of non-destructive editing because they let users manage the visibility, blending modes, and opacity of numerous objects, such as text, pictures, or modifications. Layer management enables users to perform intricate adjustments with remarkable precision. All of the tools required to create, merge, and remove layers are included in the Panel Bin.

- **Effects and Filters:** By providing users with access to a large number of pre-made effects and filters, the Panel Bin facilitates editing in Quick Mode. With these one-click effects, you can instantly alter the appearance of an image by adding creative techniques like pencil drawings or oil painting effects, or by giving it a vintage appearance. Before applying any of the many effects, users may see how they will appear in their images.

- Sharpness, brightness, contrast, and color balance are just a few of the typical adjustments that can be easily made to images using the Adjustments menu. You may adjust images using these tools to highlight details, correct lighting problems, or enhance colors. Everybody can easily utilize the Panel Bin's modifications. They include easy-to-understand controls and sliders that even novices can operate effectively.

- Frames, Textures, and Graphics: Photoshop Elements also allows you to include frames, textures, and graphics in images. You may alter and add a library of graphic components and frames to a photo using the Panel Bin to improve its appearance or add something special. Holiday frames, graphic overlays such as stars or patterns, and textures that may be applied to an image's backdrop to provide depth are just a few of the possibilities available to users.

- **Guided Edits get:** Users may get step-by-step instructions by using the shortcuts to Guided Edits in both Quick and Advanced Modes found in the Panel Bin. From simple changes like removing imperfections to more complex effects like creating a double exposure or adding text to an image, guided edits are an excellent learning tool since they lead users through particular approaches.

The Panel Bin's Flexibility

One of the best features of the Panel Bin is its flexibility to be customized. In order to concentrate on the tools they need most at any given moment, users may adjust its size or make certain components smaller. This provides you choices so that you may easily use the tools you use most often and maintain a clean workplace.

The Toolbox

The Toolbox, one of the most crucial components of Adobe Photoshop Elements, provides users with access to a vast array of tools necessary for picture creation and editing. You may execute a variety of tasks in the Toolbox on the left side of the interface for more complex editing tasks including retouching, selection, and manipulation. To be as creative as possible using Photoshop Elements, you must learn how to utilize all of the various tools in the Toolbox.

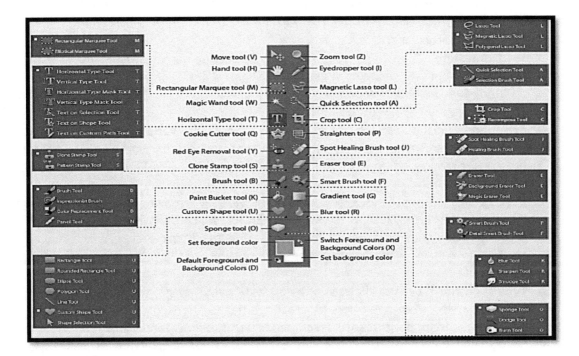

The Photoshop Elements Toolbox's Essential Tools

- **Selection Tools:** These tools are crucial for the majority of editing tasks since they allow you to work on specific areas of a picture. The Toolbox in Photoshop Elements has a number of selecting tools, including
    - ➢ **Elliptical and Rectangular Marquee Tool:** To pick out basic, geometric portions of an image.
    - ➢ **Lasso Tool:** This tool allows you to trace around irregular shapes and create freehand selections.
    - ➢ **Magic Wand Tool:** By choosing regions of a picture according to how similar their colors are, you may quickly separate things with uniform hues, such as skies or backdrops.
    - ➢ **Quick Selection Tool:** By identifying edges in a picture, the Quick Selection Tool utilizes AI to pick intricate regions with a few clicks.
- **Crop and Straighten Tools:** To improve the composition, you may use the Crop Tool to resize and crop your image, eliminating unnecessary portions. Using a line you draw across the image, the Straighten Tool automatically corrects the angle to help you straighten out crooked photographs.

- Photoshop Elements has a number of healing and retouching techniques that may be used to correct imperfections or alter portraits:
  - **Spot Healing Brush:** This tool automatically eliminates imperfections, spots, and other undesirable items by blending them with the surrounding region.
  - **Healing Brush:** Similar to the Spot Healing Brush, this brush allows you to manually mend a particular area.
  - **Clone Stamp Tool:** This tool transfers pixels between areas of an image. It may be used to duplicate elements or get rid of things.
  - **Red Eye Removal Tool:** Rapidly eliminates red eyes brought on by flash photography.
- **Brush and Pencil Tools:** The ability to paint images with various colors and textures makes the Brush Tool one of Photoshop Elements' most helpful tools. You may alter the brush's size, shape, and opacity to achieve various effects. The Pencil Tool is excellent for drawing or outlining since it is stiffer and produces precise lines and curves.
- **Eraser Tools:** This tool "erases" portions of your work by removing pixels from an image. There are other types, such as the backdrop Eraser, which removes the backdrop while preserving the primary subject's boundaries, and the Magic Eraser, which functions similarly to a magic wand and removes large portions of the same color with a single click.
- **Type Tool:** The Type Tool allows you to add text to your image. You may choose from a variety of styles, sizes, and colors for creating titles, captions, or watermarks. The Type Tool is required for projects such as scrapbook pages, memes, and signs.
- **Shape Tool:** With the Shape Tool, you can create pre-made rectangles, ellipses, and lines in addition to bespoke forms like stars or arrows. Because they are vector-based, shapes may be scaled without sacrificing quality. They are thus excellent for usage as graphic design components or borders.
- **Paint Bucket and Gradient Tools:** The Gradient Tool allows you to create creative effects or backdrops by smoothly switching between colors. In contrast, the Paint Bucket Tool applies a solid color to a region depending on the pixels you click on. It works well for solidifying backgrounds or bringing color to certain regions.
- **Zoom and Move Tools:**
  - **Move Tool:** This crucial tool allows you to rearrange layers or other picture components. This tool is often used to align design features or organize composite pieces.
  - **Zoom Tool:** As the name implies, this tool allows you to zoom in and out of your image to enhance your editing experience by highlighting certain elements.
- **Hand Tool:** You can move the Hand Tool around an image without altering its contents when you zoom in on it. It comes in handy when working in areas with a lot of detail and you need to switch your perspective without altering the zoom level.
- **Customizable settings:** You may alter a set of settings seen in the Toolbox's top menu for every tool. You may alter size, hardness, opacity, and other parameters using these

choices. By selecting these options, you can ensure that every tool is ideal for your editing requirements.

The photo bin

An effective tool for seeing, organizing, and switching between open photographs in the editing area is Adobe Photoshop Elements' Photo Bin. It's particularly helpful as a navigation tool while working on many images at once. The Photo Bin, which displays thumbnails of the images you are presently selecting, is located close to the bottom of the workspace. **This eliminates the need to open and close several windows in order to arrange them and choose the one you want to work on.**

- **Thumbnails for Simple Navigation:** The primary function of the Photo Bin is to display thumbnails of every photo you have open in Photoshop Elements. Keeping track of many projects at once and rapidly switching between images is made simple by this visual overview. You may choose any thumbnail in the bin to concentrate on a specific picture in the main editing window. This is particularly useful for integrating pieces from disparate photographs or contrasting edits.
- The Photo Bin's drag and drop feature makes it simple to move images into the workspace, onto a canvas for compositing, or into a group for side-by-side editing. This flexibility comes in quite handy when organizing or working on projects that include a lot of photographs.
- **Interaction with Layers and Projects:** In Advanced Mode, the Photo Bin plays a more intricate function by linking open photographs to the Layers panel. For instance, you may drag an image from the Photo Bin onto the current project's canvas, and it will immediately show up as a new layer. For tasks like picture compositing, which require combining many photos, this functionality is crucial. Managing projects with several levels is made simpler and faster by moving photos between the bin and layers.
- **Changing Open Files:** The Photo Bin facilitates switching between open projects or files without requiring you to shut the others. Switching between activities is made simple by these characteristics; you may modify one image, go quickly to another, and then return to the original one without losing your work or having to reopen files.
- **Fast Access to Saved Albums:** Users of the Elements Organizer may explore albums and picture collections quickly with the picture Bin. The Photo Bin allows you to see and access whole albums. This makes choosing images to edit from a bigger collection simple. When working on themed projects, such as photo albums or slideshows that have a large number of related images, this is incredibly beneficial.

You may use the following procedures to make the Photo Bin visible even if it isn't initially displayed:

- From the top of the workspace, drag down a little.
- Move the pointer over the lower-right corner.
- Pull up when the double-headed arrows show up.

CHAPTER FOUR
KEYBOARD SHORTCUTS FOR PHOTOSHOP ELEMENTS

File Management

- **New (Ctrl + N):** Create a new document.
- **Open File (Ctrl + O):** Open an existing file from your computer.
- **Close (Ctrl + W):** Close the current document.
- **Save (Ctrl + S):** Save changes to your document.
- **Save As (Ctrl + Shift + S):** Save the current document with a new name or location.
- **Save for Web (Ctrl + Shift + Alt + S):** Export your document optimized for web use.
- **Print (Ctrl + P):** Open the print dialog to print your document.
- **Presets (Ctrl + K):** Open preferences or preset settings for your workspace.

Controls view

- **Zoom In (Ctrl + +):** Increase magnification of your document.
- **Zoom Out (Ctrl + -):** Decrease magnification of your document.
- **Move View (Hold Spacebar):** Temporarily switch to the hand tool to pan around the document.
- **Hide Window Panels (Tab):** Hide or show all panels and toolbars for a cleaner workspace.
- **Fit to Screen (Ctrl + 0):** Adjust the zoom so the entire image fits on your screen.
- **100% View (Ctrl + Alt + 0):** Zoom to display your image at 100% of its actual size.
- **Show/Hide Selection (Ctrl + H):** Toggle the visibility of active selections.
- **Show/Hide Rulers (Ctrl + Shift + R):** Display or hide rulers for precise alignment.
- **Show/Hide Grid (Ctrl + 3):** Show or hide a grid overlay to assist with layout.
- **Show/Hide Guides (Ctrl + 2):** Toggle visibility of guides for object alignment.
- **Fix Guides (Ctrl + Alt):** Lock or unlock guides to prevent accidental movement.

Image modifications

- **Image Size (Ctrl + Alt + I):** Change the dimensions of your image.
- **Canvas Size (Ctrl + Alt + C):** Adjust the workspace area without changing the image size.
- **Invert Colors (Ctrl + I):** Invert the colors in the current selection or entire image.
- **Tone Correction (Ctrl + L):** Adjust the tonal range using the Levels tool.
- **Intelligent Auto Correction (Ctrl + Alt + M):** Apply automatic corrections to the image for improved balance.
- **Auto Tone (Ctrl + Shift + L):** Automatically adjust tonal values.
- **Auto Contrast (Ctrl + Shift + Alt + L):** Automatically adjust contrast for a balanced image.
- **Auto Color (Ctrl + Shift + B):** Automatically correct color balance.
- **Black & White (Ctrl + Alt + B):** Convert your image to grayscale.
- **Hue/Saturation (Ctrl + U):** Adjust the hue, saturation, and lightness of the image.
- **Desaturate (Ctrl + Shift + U):** Remove all color from the image to create a grayscale effect.

Tools selection

- **Select All (Ctrl + A):** Select the entire image or layer.
- **Deselect (Ctrl + D):** Cancel the current selection.
- **Reselect (Ctrl + Shift + D):** Reapply the previous selection.
- **Invert Selection (Ctrl + Shift + I):** Invert the current selection to select everything else.
- **Feather Selection (Ctrl + Alt + D):** Smooth the edges of your selection for a soft transition.

Management of layer

- **New Layer (Ctrl + Shift + N):** Create a new blank layer.
- **Duplicate Layer (Ctrl + J):** Make a copy of the active layer.
- **Create Clipping Mask (Ctrl + G):** Restrict one layer's visibility to the contents of another.
- **Merge Layers (Ctrl + E):** Merge the selected layer with the one below it.
- **Flatten Image (Ctrl + Shift + E):** Merge all visible layers into one.
- **Delete Layer (Delete key or Ctrl + J):** Remove the selected layer from the document.
- **Hide Layer Mask (Shift + Click on Mask):** Temporarily hide a layer mask.
- **Show Layer Mask (Alt + Click on Mask):** View the layer mask by itself.
- **Opacity Adjustment (1 - 0):** Quickly change the layer opacity from 10% to 100% by pressing number keys.
- **Change Blending Mode (Shift + +/-):** Cycle through different blending modes for the active layer.
- **Select Specific Blending Mode (Alt + Shift + [letter]):** Shortcut to jump directly to a specific blending mode (e.g., Alt + Shift + N for Normal).

Shortcuts for blending mode

- **Normal (Alt + Shift + N):** Regular blending with no interaction between layers.
- **Dissolve (Alt + Shift + I):** Blends with a dissolving, speckled effect.
- **Darken (Alt + Shift + K):** Keeps the darkest pixels and ignores lighter ones.
- **Multiply (Alt + Shift + M):** Multiplies the color values, darkening the image.
- **Color Burn (Alt + Shift + B):** Burns the image colors, resulting in a more intense effect.
- **Linear Burn (Alt + Shift + A):** Darkens the image while retaining highlights.
- **Lighten (Alt + Shift + G):** Blends by keeping the lightest pixels.
- **Screen (Alt + Shift + S):** Multiplies the inverse of the layer colors, resulting in a brighter effect.
- **Color Dodge (Alt + Shift + D):** Lightens the image by dodging the color values.
- **Linear Dodge (Alt + Shift + W):** Brightens the image more smoothly than regular dodge.

- **Overlay (Alt + Shift + O):** Combines multiply and screen effects for contrast.
- **Soft Light (Alt + Shift + F):** A softer version of overlay, with less intense effects.
- **Hard Light (Alt + Shift + H):** A more intense contrast between light and dark areas.
- **Vivid Light (Alt + Shift + V):** Dramatically boosts contrast and color.
- **Linear Light (Alt + Shift + J):** Combines linear dodge and burn for strong lighting effects.
- **Pin Light (Alt + Shift + Z):** Replaces colors depending on their lightness or darkness.
- **Hard Mix (Alt + Shift + L):** Adds higher contrast by reducing color gradients.
- **Difference (Alt + Shift + E):** Highlights the difference between two layers.
- **Exclusion (Alt + Shift + X):** Similar to difference but with less contrast.
- **Hue (Alt + Shift + U):** Blends only the hue of one layer with another.
- **Saturation (Alt + Shift + T):** Uses the saturation of one layer on another.
- **Color (Alt + Shift + C):** Combines the hue and saturation from one layer with the luminance of another.
- **Luminance (Alt + Shift + Y):** Blends the luminance values, useful for black-and-white images.

Apply filters

- **Apply Last Filter (Ctrl + F):** Reapply the last used filter.
- **Modify Last Filter Settings (Ctrl + Alt + F):** Reopen the last filter's dialog box to adjust settings.

Tools for toolbar

- **Lasso (L):** Freehand selection tool.
- **Magnetic Lasso (L):** Automatically snaps to the edges of objects.
- **Polygonal Lasso (L):** Create straight-edged selections.
- **Crop Tool (C):** Crop the image to your desired size.
- **Spot Healing Brush (J):** Quickly remove blemishes or unwanted details.
- **Eraser (E):** Erase parts of a layer.
- **Smart Brush (F):** Automatically adjusts specific areas with pre-set effects.
- **Blur Tool (R):** Softens specific areas.
- **Dodge Tool (O):** Lightens specific areas.
- **Rectangular Marquee (M):** Select rectangular areas.
- **Ellipse Marquee (M):** Select elliptical areas.
- **Brush Tool (B):** Paints on your image using the selected brush settings.
- **Text Tool (T):** Add horizontal or vertical text.
- **Clone Stamp (S):** Copy and stamp pixels from one part of the image to another.
- **Shape Tool (U):** Draw vector shapes like rectangles, ellipses, lines, and more.

CHAPTER FIVE
GETTING YOUR PHOTOS ORGANIZED

An Overview of the Elements Organizer

Adobe Photoshop Elements' key feature is the Elements Organizer, which makes it easier to organize, sort, and access to your photographs and movies. Anyone with a large number of media files may utilize it with ease. It makes your job simpler by enabling you to easily organize, categorize, and locate your files—especially whether you're simply capturing images for pleasure or are new to photo editing.

Important Features

- **Material Management:** All of your digital material is stored in The Organizer, which makes it simple to upload images and videos, arrange them, and locate them fast. Because it supports a wide range of file formats, it is a versatile option for both picture and video tags. To make things simpler to discover, you may create albums, group relevant material, and categorize files.

- **Smart Tags & Auto-Curation:** One of the finest features of the Organizer is the usage of AI-powered smart tags and auto-curation. Depending on what your material includes, the program may automatically categorize it with the appropriate tags. For example, it can automatically add the tags "beach" and "birthday" to your vacation or family images. By selecting the finest images from a collection based on factors like composition, lighting, and clarity, auto-curation goes one step further. This greatly expedites the sorting process.

- **Facial Recognition:** The Organizer's sophisticated facial recognition technology makes it simpler to locate images of certain individuals. You may sort and organize photos by person after the program recognizes faces in your collection and knows who is in each image.

- **Instant Search:** Using tags, dates, locations, and other features, users may locate certain images with the aid of the features Organizer's robust Instant Search function. Photographers may also search by categories, such as camera models or settings, if they want to focus their search.

- **Geotagging and Places View:** Places View allows users to browse their images by location, regardless of whether they were shot manually or with a GPS-enabled device. With geotagging, users may add locations to images. This application is excellent for vacation photography since it allows users to categorize photographs on a map according to where they were shot.

- **Event View:** This tool may help you better manage your media by allowing you to group files according to significant occasions such as family gatherings, marriages, birthdays, and holidays. The ability to associate images with events helps you recall significant occasions in the future.

- **People View:** This specialist view arranges photos according to the individuals they include. The Organizer can automatically add pictures of friends and family to groups using facial recognition technology. This makes it simple to locate images of certain individuals.

Usability

Even those who have never used the Elements Organizer before may quickly and easily use it since Adobe designed it as simple as possible. The UI, which has drag-and-drop capability and guided training for those unfamiliar with digital organizing tools, is simple to use. The program also works nicely with Photoshop Elements and Premiere Elements for those that utilize both photo and video editing tools.

Connectivity to Mobile Apps and Creative Cloud

Elements Organizer is also compatible with Adobe's Creative Cloud and mobile applications. Images from your phone, cloud storage, or social network accounts may be added straight to the organizer. It will be simpler to access and modify your material across a range of platforms and devices.

Compatibility and Versions

Adobe continuously adds new functionality and enhancements to the Elements Organizer. The 2025 version features stronger AI support, is more compatible with the Apple M3 chip, and organizes larger picture and video collections more easily overall. Even users of more recent media and devices will have a seamless experience since it supports a wide variety of file formats.

Using the Elements Organizer to import media

Images are never copied into the Elements Organizer; instead, they are "imported" into the application. When you say "import," you just indicate that they are connected to the Organizer from their storage location, which is often the Pictures folder. Perhaps Elements has a problem and has to be reloaded if that link is broken. Elements will immediately re-link all of your files, and you can quickly restore the catalog from a backup. Sometimes the application has to be pointed to the disk containing the images, but most of the time; Elements will search for and locate every image that was linked in the catalog. It's a clever tool.

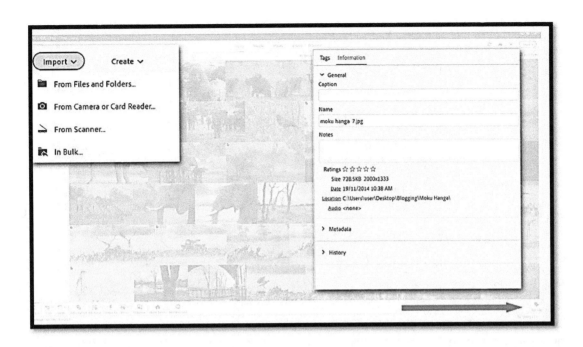

Import: You may immediately import photos, music, or video clips into the Elements Organizer by selecting the From Files and Folders... option from the Import button, which is located in the upper left-hand corner of the Organizer. These files may reside elsewhere, such as locally or on a USB device; they are never really "in" Elements. Additionally, you may import a large number of files at once from pre-organized folders or straight from a card reader or camera. The panel on the right side of the main window contains search phrases and additional information about each file. Click the little Keyword/Info button (with the arrow on the screen) to open or close this panel. Because of the linking procedure, it is not a good idea to relocate or modify the names of files that have already been "imported" into Elements. If a file has been relocated or renamed, Elements will notify you that it is missing the next time it starts up and will start searching for it right away.

If the name stays the same, this is OK. However, it will need to be imported once again if the name changes. If the file was simply transferred to a new disk or folder, you may either let Elements search for it or, if you know where the file was moved, do it yourself. The number of photographs you have will determine how long it takes Elements to locate a file you transferred. Elements merely replicate the information, which is mostly text and thumbnails when you connect to the source files. This speeds up the import procedure. Before importing the files into the organizer, it is preferable to arrange them on your computer or external storage. You will avoid wasting time searching for files that were relocated or renamed after they were imported in this method. Each of us has a distinct setup for our hectic photography life. While some choose to organize their files by date, others like to name them after significant occasions in their life. This may be done as you choose. The method you can remember is the greatest.

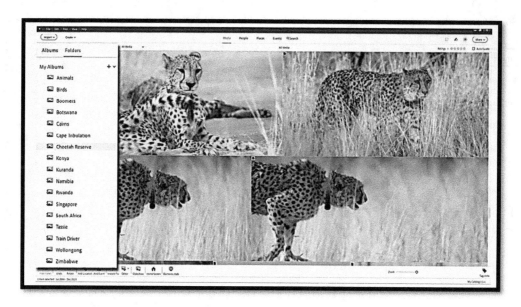

Album creation: I created the "Animals" album seen in the top picture. The contents of the album will be shown in the main window if you click on the album on the left side of the window. Like the majority of other Elements features, you may alter an album's name at any moment. The ability to save the same picture or photographs in several albums without using up more hard disk space is a major advantage of creating albums. Not only that, but it also lets you swiftly break up your work into smaller, more manageable groupings.

The first set of pictures should be arranged before the second set is added. The main panel can soon become clogged with hundreds of photographs if you keep importing folder after folder of pictures, which may be quite confusing. After importing files into the Organizer, you may view the precise location of those files on your hard drives by using the Folders menu in the left-hand bin.

Auto Curate: There are several useful capabilities in Photoshop Elements that aren't typically used. Among them is Auto Curate, which selects the 500 finest photos from the Organizer and is located in the upper right corner of the screen. What you discover may surprise you. Adobe claims that Elements will choose 50 of the finest photographs from a total of 20,000 images after you have your media in the main window and tick the "Auto Curate" option. It's odd that it selects 50 of my test media's finest images—or any other number you choose. In any case, I believe the most of them are decent. Still, this is worth a look if you want a fast and simple choice.

- After making changes to anything, give it a suitable name.
- The main window will display newly added photographs from the Organizer. To enlarge or reduce the size of the images, use the zoom slider located in the lower right corner of the screen. To go down the page and see further thumbnails, you may use the edge-of-screen sliders or the up and down arrow keys on your computer.

All of the details about this filing system, including albums, tags, keywords, thumbnails, original files, and more, are available in the Elements catalog. The backup location for this catalog must be distinct from the location of the original files.

Getting your job organized: Images with a star rating

The Windows operating system's star ratings may be familiar to some of you. Using this tool, you may rate a file from one to five stars according to its quality. Following that, you may search for files (in this example, images) with X stars. You might assign three stars to photos that need editing and five stars to your greatest images. Numerous picture editing applications, including Adobe Bridge, Lightroom, and the picture Mechanic image viewer from Camera Bits, have ratings. This is due to the method's ease of use and ability to maintain organization.

To do this, take the following actions:

1. In the Organizer, right-click a picture.
2. Locate the Ratings option in step two, then slide over the star rating (ranging from 1 to 5) you want to assign to that image. Press any key from 1 to 5 (not the number pad) after selecting one or more images in the main window to add a rating.
3. Click the star symbol in the Ratings search bar (located at the top of the page, just under the Create tab) to locate an image that has previously been rated. Everything with that rating will remain unchanged on the main screen. Only after you click on the same star rating once again to terminate the search will you be able to view anything else. You may narrow down your search by selecting Greater than, or equal to, less than, or equal to, or rating is equivalent to by clicking on the little icon to the right of Ratings. Your search results may change significantly as a consequence. This approach is excellent at producing outcomes and is extremely easy to comprehend, set up, and modify. Simply decrease, increase, or remove the rating using the pop-out menu if necessary.

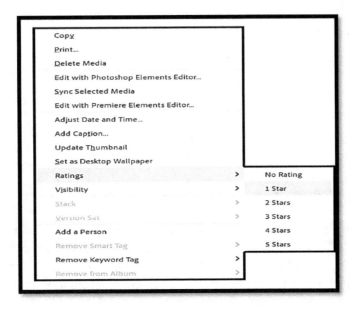

31

Contextual menu assistance: When browsing through newly imported photographs, it's a good idea to develop the habit of right-clicking a thumbnail. This brings up an extensive contextual menu. You may choose from the following options to sort images: Remove from the Catalog, Edit with Premiere Elements Editor, Photoshop Elements Editor, Add a person to the picture to aid in future searches, add a caption, add ratings (1–5 stars), and change the date and time (helpful when switching time zones). When several picture thumbnails are selected, create a Slideshow and Show File Info to see the file's information. All is well.

Getting your job organized: Metadata-based image search

When you snap a photo, all the information about your camera is stored in a little text file called metadata. Unless we are specifically searching for it—in this example, seeking for images—metadata is often not read. In addition to the date, time, filename, size, resolution, and, if your camera has them, GPS coordinates, metadata also records details about the camera and lens. Because metadata is pre-existing, I can utilize Organizer to quickly search our picture database using any of the previously recorded metadata information. The Find by Details (Metadata) search box allows you to search for images in a variety of methods, which may be confusing to you. Additionally, you may store frequently performed searches in this dialog box, which can save you a great deal of time. If you are on vacation and in several time zones, this is very helpful. You may search for pictures based on the time and date of their capture.

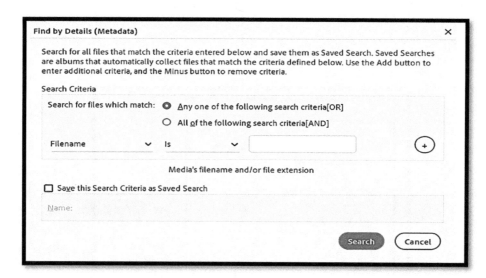

Metadata search: This page appears when you choose Find > By Details (Metadata). It begins by searching for files that meet any of the following search parameters (by capture date, which you may choose using the drop-down menu) when it first opens. To see 36 other search options, click the menu on the left. This kind of search is really wide. I often look up particular terms like aperture (f-stop), ISO setting, focal length, and white balance since I write a lot about

32

photography procedures. This facilitates the process of sorting through hundreds of potential image files. I also often utilize the kind of camera or the date shot as a search criteria. However, you may use any of Elements' other search criteria, including individuals tags, Event tags, and keywords, for instance, if you wish to discover individuals. If what is on the menu isn't particular enough, you may add a second or third "search rule" by clicking the plus symbol (+) to the right of the Search Criteria window.

Quick information: Tags in the right-hand panel and the Information panel in this image share space. There is a short version and an expanded version, and the larger version now occupies the most of the right-hand panel. It is rather extensive. Above that is the General menu, which in this case is hovering above the tree snake's primary image. This displays the file's star rating, location on your hard drives, and some of its information. It's interesting to note that the data shown here isn't as comprehensive as that found in the Find menu, but it's still a decent place to start looking.

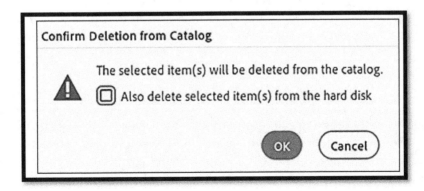

One tip is to right-click on a thumbnail and choose "Delete from Catalog," which will cause a box to appear asking whether you also want to remove the actual file from it. If you are certain that it must go, this is useful!

Hint: As you grow more particular, you may take keywording as far as you have time and patience. For example, I might keyword my trip images with "beaches," "restaurants," "funny signs," "people," "markets," "nightlife," "sunsets," "palm trees," and "cocktails." Make sure you use a comma (,) between each term if you add several keywords so the search engine doesn't get confused. Each image should include no more than five or six keywords. Excessive keyword use might be detrimental.

Putting your work in order: Using keywords

Elements' ability to search through hundreds, thousands, or even tens of thousands of images using keyword tags is one of its finest features. Click on a file once to pick it while seeing a fresh collection of images, and then input a keyword in the lower right corner of the screen.

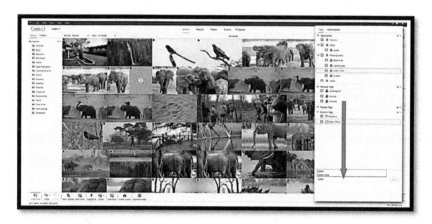

Keyword tagging: As you can see behind the red arrow, I entered in the term "Safari." This way, if I upload hundreds of African wildlife photos into the Organizer and add keywords to them, I just need to click on the Safari tag (highlighted in blue above) to locate those images. They may then be included in "Safari" (or whatever your project is) as an album. One of the most crucial aspects of configuring this application, in my opinion, is adding keywords to anything you import into the Organizer. You can search for and locate nearly any image weeks, months, or even years later if you do this on a regular basis. It's a highly effective and efficient method of obtaining photos. You just returned from a trip. Select every photo from the trip and enter the location's name. For instance, if you visited Australia, you could keyword all of the photos with "Australia." However, if you spent half of your time in the mountains near Katoomba, you should re-select those photos and add "Katoomba" as the keyword. You can quickly keyword all the significant events in this album (called "Holiday in Australia") if you plan ahead. If you spent three days surfing in Australia, re-select those photos and add the keyword "surfing." This will only take a few minutes. In this manner, you can search for "Australia," "surfing," or "cocktails,"

34

for instance, and Elements will locate those images (almost) instantly in the months or years that follow.

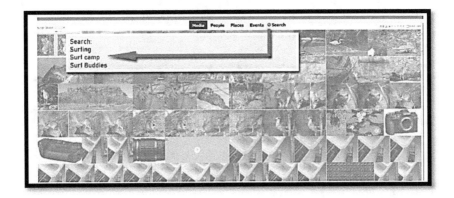

Practice searching: In the Search field (the blue magnifying glass icon, shown here with an arrow) on the Organizer screen, type in a location or event and pertinent keywords (such as "Surfing" or "Australia"), and the program will immediately locate the images. Because it simply needs to search through its database, which consists mostly of text entries, rather than terabytes of high-resolution RAW files, it operates rapidly.

Customizing Tags: I chose Edit from the contextual menu that displayed when I right-clicked on the Bali keyword tag in the right-hand bin of this picture. When you do this, the Edit Keyword Tag window appears here, on the left. You have the option to change the tag name in addition to adding comments. A larger window will open in the center if you click on the Edit Icon tab. To make it easier to identify, you can include a picture of a Balinese group here. Although it's a cute feature, it won't help you accomplish anything. When you attempt to locate particular pictures from that trip, the magic begins. Keywording is a straightforward procedure. The file has built-in keyword tags so that, for example, if I sent someone a collection of my tagged photos, they could use the tags I added to sort them. The tags in Elements can be read by many other apps that edit images. The only thing that Elements can accomplish, however, is an album. In the right-hand tag bin, you can create a new tag. Simply drag the tag across the image's thumbnail to apply it to an image. Simple. Drag the new tag onto any thumbnail you've chosen after selecting all 100 photos if you need to add the same tag to them. All of the photos you chose will immediately have the new tag applied. Very clever!

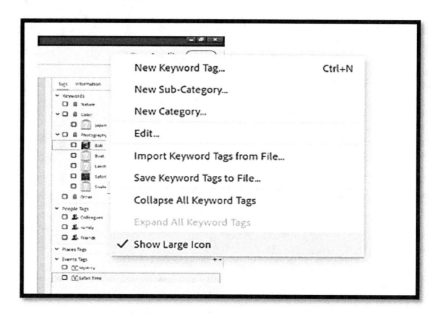

Tag management: I've made the pop-out Tags menu larger in this picture to display all of its choices. This has everything you need to label everything you add to Elements. Pay special attention to how you tag images, and you'll never lose another one. Also, bear in mind that the plus marks (+) always signify that you may add a new feature, whether they are in the Tags bin or someplace else in this program. You may use this example to build a new keyword tag, category, or subcategory. You may also use it to import tags from a file, save tags to a file, or adjust the tag structure by making it larger or smaller.

Organizing your work: Places

Many elements in the Organizer are geared to help photographers discover and keep track of their images. That being said, I believe there are too many search options. Places feature has been a part of Elements for a long time. Its major function is to rapidly upload any photo with GPS data to a globe map that is linked to the internet. This manner, viewers may readily identify photographs by viewing where they were shot. Many cameras didn't have GPS capabilities in previous editions of this application (many years ago), therefore the only way to achieve this type of presentation was to "pin" photographs on the map from the grid on the left side of the screen. You can still do this.

There are two methods to see the feature: pinned and unpinned. In the second mode, you may choose one or more images and drag them to the location where they were shot, which will mark them on the map. As soon as they are pinned, they show up on the Pinned tab. If you chose the incorrect position, you may merely drag the saved image(s) to a new spot. The stored picture thumbnails will open in Grid view if you double-click on them. Double-clicking them again will cause them to open in full screen. On paper, places seem like a great feature, but not many people actually utilize them. This, I believe, is due to the fact that few cameras save GPS information.

Note: No one has ever explained why locations haven't functioned in previous iterations of Elements before 2018. However, now that it's all rectified, Places will function flawlessly in Elements 2025.

Planning your work: Activities

I feel that frequent photographers will find the Events category more helpful. Why? Events begin by classifying photographs depending on dates. I could snap a lot of images over a family weekend or our 12-day vacation to Bali. With the Events feature, these photographs may be placed together into events that are established by the data or the metadata, or they can be put together and given a more memorable name, like "Bali Vacation" or "Family Weekend, 2019."

Workplace events: This picture demonstrates the value of sorting by date. The Number of Groups slider is located on the left-hand side (highlighted in red) of the Events window at the bottom. The search engine is speeding up time by pushing everything against everything else. Almost daily photographs are shown in the center window (highlighted in blue) if you move the slider to the right. Finding images from a day shoot or other brief event is much simpler as a result. The front pane displays the named events in the Named tab (highlighted in orange). Things may change. Named and suggested are the two view styles for events. In general, I don't appreciate anything that attempt to tell me what to do, like predictive text. But in this situation, it displays all of your images arranged by date. This is incredibly useful since it rapidly organizes everything in the main window, whether it's from an album, a folder, or all of your media. That's a solid start. Right-click on an Event and choose "Remove this Event" to remove an Event. Editing the event (adding or deleting photographs from the event) is accessible from this pop-out menu. Set as Cover makes the picture presented as the default front page, and Create a Slideshow puts all the files in that event stack into a slideshow that can be saved for further editing in the Organizer or published straight to social media using the Share option (top right corner of the Organizer).

Give that event a name: Click the "Add Event" button at the bottom of the page after making your selection. When you do this, a dialog box will appear where you can name the event, check the dates, choose a group if needed, and provide a description if needed. Lastly, click "OK" to save the modifications. It's a good idea to give albums and folders actual names rather than merely dates. Places may be used in the same way. Use the Number of Groups slider to display your event in a single collection of pictures. Holding using the Shift key, click on the first and final image in the group to physically pick all of those images. All of them have been chosen. You just need to put a marquee around each set of photographs to choose more than one. However, what becomes to the correct names that were just applied to this collection of images? All of the images you named and altered will now appear as stacked thumbnails if you choose the

Named tab at the top of the page. The elements in a group are shown when the cursor is moved over it. Double-clicking on an event stack reveals the images it contains. On the same screen, clicking the "Back" button will restore the stacked arrangement of those dispersed images.

Advice: Click and drag the cursor over each image you wish to have appeared when creating a marquee. A rectangle will result from this. Blue checkmarks indicate which items are selected. The image you missed can be added by holding down the Ctrl or Command key while you click the mouse once (Mac/Windows). Similarly, if you accidentally select too many files, you can deselect them by clicking on them while holding down Ctrl or Cmd. As your photo collection expands, you can further refine your search or just what is displayed in the main window by selecting different dates from the calendar that is displayed on the right side of the screen. Additionally, you can create a new event in the media window. Click the "Add Event" tab at the bottom of the page. After that, drag the images you wish to use in the new event to the bin on the right. Click OK after giving it a suitable name and verifying the date.

Putting your work in order: People

The "People" mode in Elements is all about facial recognition. When images are first added to the organizer, it looks at them in the background using an algorithm. If it finds a face in an image, it displays it as a circular thumbnail in the People window. If it believes there are multiple instances of the same individual in the import, it will stack them like a deck of cards. The "Unnamed" panel displays the outcomes. The label "Add Name" will appear beneath the thumbnail at the beginning of each image. Enter the name of the person in the photo in the "Add Name" field if you know them. Clicking the check mark to the right of the field to lock it in causes the picture stack to disappear.

The People window is this. Elements can be instructed to search through your image collections and quickly identify any that contain people. It's excellent, but it will make mistakes, so you'll typically need to make some minor edits to make it look flawless. Where has it disappeared to? The newly named stack will appear when you click into the Named window. The words "Faces or Photos" will appear if you move your mouse pointer over the stack. You can view the entire photo where the face was located by selecting Photos. You will only see that face or faces in that group if you click Faces. In Elements, the "People" window will locate images of your friends as well as any image that appears to be a face, such as images on posters or abstract backgrounds. To disable these, simply right-click on the button and select "Don't show again." When you name an image, it goes to the Named tab and stacks with other images that share the same name. For those of us who prefer to identify our photos by their subject matter—more especially, the individuals they feature—the People tool is incredibly useful.

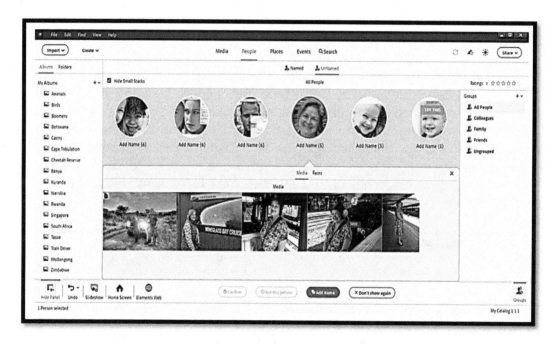

Organizing your people: As you can see on the right side of the screen, the People feature (pictured here) allows you to group your discovered faces into more manageable categories, much like the keywords feature does. By default, Elements assigns you three groups: Friends, Family, and Colleagues. You can simply click the green plus (+) symbol if you need to add more. You can use a straightforward strategy and just use keywords or ratings, as is the case with most of Elements' organizational tools, or you can combine all of the topics we've covered here to create a sophisticated database that is highly searchable. The best advice is to decide how you want to arrange your photos before you begin. Instead of having to go back and make changes to everything that was already in the Organizer because you changed your mind, you can start saving time right away. Planning will save you a great deal of time and effort.

Advice: You can merge files into a single stack by clicking and dragging them over one another. Stacks can be added to groups, such as "Family," to improve the sorting process. Click the Groups tab in the lower right corner of the main window. By clicking the green plus sign, you can either create a new group or use one of the pre-made ones. You can have as many groups as you like, just like with many other Elements features. If a face is "inappropriate" in the stack, you can either rename it or right-click the Faces icon or select "Not..." As a result, the face is now in a different stack from the original stack. Additionally, you may utilize this pop-out option to set that image as your profile picture (it is the default top of the stack). By selecting "Don't Show Again," the last option, the image will never appear in the "People" view again.

Saving your files

It is important to keep in mind that when you choose the "Save" option (File>Save) to save a JPEG, TIFF, PSD, or PNG file, certain older applications may write the new file on top of the old one, erasing the old one and storing the (ideally) better. In contrast, Elements always asks whether it's OK to replace the old version of the file, which might save you face in some circumstances. When you open a file, choose File>Save without making any changes to it. This won't do anything since it won't save the file. It will display the Save as panel, however, if you make any changes to the file and then choose File>Save.

This may be used for the following purposes:
- Save your progress.
- Modify the file format if necessary.
- The saved file should be added back to the organizer.
- Make a duplicate of it, such as NewPortrait copy.jpg.
- Create a Version Set by saving it (see overleaf).

⊥ It may be saved using a particular color profile.

The helpful function "Save to the Cloud" was removed in 2022 after being introduced in Elements 2021. It is compatible with both the Web and mobile companion apps, and it is set in 2024. The Advanced Edit or Organizer windows provide access to this capability. Although this cloud browser allows you to create collages and presentations, it is now only accessible in beta form in English. Elements will display a warning window (seen above with a caution symbol) asking whether you want to stop without saving if you make changes to the file and then attempt to end it by pressing Ctrl/Cmd + W. This is only for added security. You can select Yes, No, or Cancel.

Saving Version Sets

Another option in the Save As box is to Save as a Copy and Save in Version Set with Original. The first feature allows you to save your cherry blossom photo in both its original and updated versions. The only picture you can see in Organizer is the original. However, if you right-click on it, all of the other copies you've created from it will be visible. This file contains single images arranged like a deck of cards, piled on top of one another. It's called a Version Set. If you need to, you can add more versions or get rid of old ones. It saves screen room because everything is kept in one file.

The Effects and Adjustments features in Elements provide me lots of opportunity to experiment with various types of special effects, which are something I like. Version Sets could be just what you need to keep all of those different variants of a theme secure in one file until you choose which one to use.

CHAPTER SIX
ESSENTIAL PHOTO EDITING

Image Cropping and Straightening

Cropping a Picture

Despite the advancements in camera technology, it is still uncommon to capture a photo with the horizon line completely level or the objects properly balanced. In the Editor, there are two fast and simple methods for cropping your photos.

Cropping a picture using the Crop tool

- Choose the Crop tool from the toolbox or press C to enter Quick or Advanced mode.

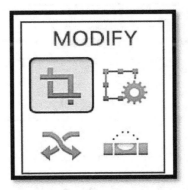

- To see the tool's instant suggestions, move the mouse over the Crop Suggestions thumbnails in the Tool Options bar. To adjust the crop, click on one. Or, to specify the portion of the picture you want to preserve, drag in the image window.

To show you what will be erased, the picture outside the selected region becomes darker.

- You may change the size of your selection by dragging the handle on one of the eight handles on its edges after moving the pointer over it.

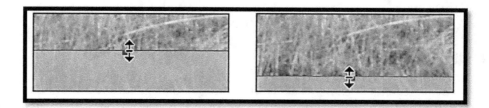

To recompose the displayed content, you may also drag within the selection.

- If you're not content with your choice, click the Cancel option to start again.

Double-click within the selection, hit Enter or Return, or click the Commit button (the checkmark) in the selection's lower-right corner if you're satisfied with the crop area.

The picture is cropped by the editor to fit the region you choose.

A Crop option features an overlay that splits the area into thirds to aid with photo composition. To modify this instruction, choose a different Grid Overlay button from the Tool Options box. You may choose the Crop tool shield's color and opacity settings in the Display & Cursors section of the Preferences window. Your cropped selection is surrounded by this muted region. By default, the opacity level is 75% and the color is black.

Resolution and Cropping

To adjust an image's size to a certain size using the Crop tool:

- Use the last section's steps 1 through 3 to choose an area to crop.
- Select a normal picture size from the Crop Preset Options option in the Tool Options bar.

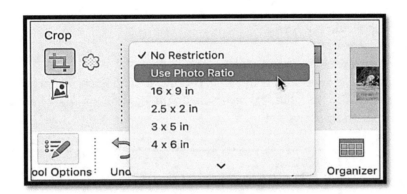

In the W (width) and H (height) sections, you may additionally provide a size. The values are altered when you hit the double-arrow button between the fields. Because of this, shifting a crop area from horizontal to vertical and back again is simple.

- Double-click within the selection, hit Enter or Return, or click the Commit button to trim the image.

To crop a picture using the Rectangular Marquee tool:

- Press M or choose the Rectangular Marquee tool from the toolbox if you are in Advanced mode.
- To specify the portion of the picture you want to save, you may drag in the image window.

- After choosing an image, choose Crop. The Editor crops the picture to suit the region you want.

Advice: Make sure you edit your photos to a standard size before using a professional print provider to print them. Prints may have black bars around the borders because digital camera image sizes don't always correspond with standard photo sizes.

Extend the Background

A photograph is often cropped to remove portions of it. However, there are occasions where expanding the viewable region is possible. The new areas are subsequently filled in by the editor using pixels from the picture's edges.

To provide further context:

- After opening an image, go to Guided mode.
- After selecting the Special Edits heading, choose "Extend Background."
- Select a canvas size from the first selection on the right. Blank spaces are put around the original image to adjust its size.

- Usually, the feature should occupy the whole expanded space. If you wish to fill just certain places, click the black arrows in the sidebar of step 2.
- When you choose the "Autofill" option, content-aware technology will complete the gaps.

To specify protected zones, you may also click the "Extend" option. This option expands the picture in unprotected regions rather than creating new pixels depending on the edges. Click "Done." to apply the extension.

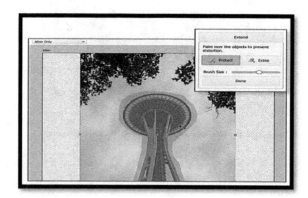

When you use Autofill (left) and extend (right), you get these results.

+ If necessary, correct spots that seem to be duplicates or don't look properly throughout the extension process by using the Spot Healing Brush or Clone Stamp Tool buttons.
+ You have the option to save the picture or continue working in Quick or Advanced mode after selecting Next.

Hint: You may easily go back in time by selecting Edit > Undo whenever you want. Click the "Reset Image" button at the top of the shelf to begin again.

Make a Crooked Photo Straight

Even the most meticulously planned photographs might be a little wrong if the horizon line is not quite level or the portrait subjects are skewed. The helpful Straighten tool makes it simple to straighten up photographs that aren't aligned correctly. Or maybe a photo you scanned shifted when you replaced the scanner cover. You may trim it to a neat rectangle if you'd like, and Elements will straighten it for you right away.

To use the Straighten tool, do the following actions:
+ Either press P or choose the Straighten tool from the Advanced mode toolbox.

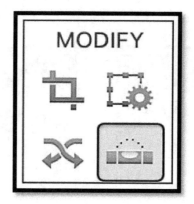

↓ After you straighten the image, you may choose how to trim it using the Tool Options bar.

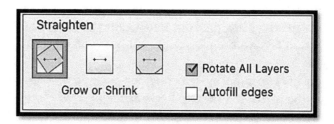

If you want the tool to fill in the blanks using Content-Aware technology, choose Autofill Edges.

↓ Using the horizon line or another subject as a reference, drag along the line. The image rotates and aligns with the newly established horizontal plane when you release the drag.

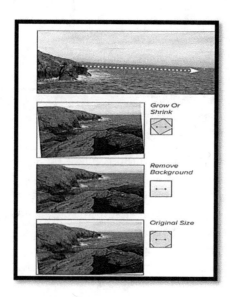

To allow the editor to correct an image: Select one of these:
- Image > Rotate > Crop and Straighten Image
- Image > Rotate > Image Straighten

The Straighten and Crop Image command will do all in its power to straighten the image and remove any extraneous background. The Straighten picture command only straightens the picture without cropping it. Both approaches have drawbacks. When there are around fifty vacant pixels surrounding the crop region, Straighten and Crop performs at its best. If the border is extremely narrow, it may be difficult for the editor to distinguish between the picture and the border. This implies that they may not be able to properly crop the image. The Straighten Image command is likely a better option since it prevents the Editor from cropping off areas of your image that you may wish to maintain, but you'll still need to crop your image manually. **To straighten a picture using the Crop tool:**
- Select the Crop tool from the toolbox.
- In the image window, drag to choose the area of the image you wants to crop and straighten.
- When you step beyond the selection area's boundary, the pointer will turn into a spinning pointer.

Rotate the selection till it aligns with the picture content once you have a general notion of where to crop.
- Drag the selection outside of it until the edges match the content of the picture.
- To adjust the placement, drag the selection handles as needed.
- Click the Confirm button or use the Enter or Return keys. The image is automatically cropped and aligned for you.

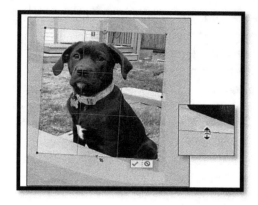

Before the photo is straightened for you by Elements, make any last adjustments you want to your cropping choices (top).

Using the Perspective Crop tool to correct distortion

You may simultaneously correct any keystone distortion and crop an image using the Perspective Crop tool. An item may seem to be a trapezoid rather than a square or rectangle if you photograph a long corridor at an angle or a towering skyscraper from below looking up. **Take these actions to simultaneously crop and correct this:**

+ After choosing a picture in Advanced mode, use the Perspective Crop tool from the Tools menu.
+ Additionally, you may hold down the C key until the tool appears. It is next to the equipment for the Crop and Cookie Cutter.
+ Click at each corner to draw a marquee around the warped picture.
+ Adjust the corners and borders of the marquee as needed. If you would like, you may choose from a variety of possibilities.
  ➤ **Width (W) and Height (H):** Select the crop's desired width and height.
  ➤ **Resolution:** Select the desired resolution for the cropped image. Don't upsample your image for the same reason as the Crop tool.
  ➤ **Pixels/in or Pixels/cm:** Select the desired unit of measurement.

➢ **Show Grid:** Activate or deactivate the image's overlaying grid of vertical and horizontal lines.

⤵ Within the cropping marquee, double-click: You may alternatively hit Enter or click the blue checkmark next to the marquee. To remove your crop, click the blue "Cancel X" button. Elements need to correct the keystone distortion and crop your image. If you are unhappy with the angle of your marquee in Step 3, adjust it by clicking Edit > Undo. Before I achieved the outcome you see below, I had to make many attempts.

Using a selected boundary for cropping

You may choose Image > Crop in either Advanced or Quick mode to crop an image in any of those modes. First, choose using any of the available tools. Next, choose the command. Any selection border shape may be used with this technique. In other words, your choice need not be square or rectangular; it might be freeform or spherical. Elements crops as near to the selected boundary as it can, but that form is not visible in the reduced image.

Rearranging Pictures

With this fantastic tool, you can resize—or, as the name implies, recompose—your picture without sacrificing any crucial elements. This tool might be useful in situations when you need to relocate people or animals closer together and crop a picture to make it squarer rather than rectangular. **How it operates:**

⤵ Choose the Recompose tool in Advanced mode from the Tools panel.

⤵ Another option is to hit W. The tool has a gear on top of a square-like form.

⤵ From the Tool Options, choose the Mark for Protection Brush. The brush with the plus sign symbol is this one. Next, apply a brush stroke to the areas of your picture that you want to save or safeguard. You may choose the brush's size using the Size option slider.

To remove any errors, use the Erase Highlights Marked for Protection tool (the eraser with the plus sign symbol).

+ Use the Mark for Removal Brush (the brush with the minus symbol) to brush over the areas of your picture that you want to remove or that aren't necessary for the finished product. You may choose the brush's size using the Size option slider. Any errors may be eliminated by using the Erase Highlights Marked for Removal tool, which is the eraser with the minus symbol.

+ Enter any other required parameters in the Tool Options. **Other choices include of:**

> **Threshold:** This slider regulates the amount of recomposing that appears in your modification. Selecting 100% results in a fully recomposed picture. Experiment until you get the desired outcomes.

> **Preset Ratios:** To have your picture framed in that size, choose one of the preset aspect ratios. "No Restriction" is another option for freedom.

> **Width and Height:** Using this option, you may adjust the image's dimensions. To prevent skin tones from warping while resizing, use the "Highlight Skin Tones" option (green man symbol).

+ To adjust the size or location of your picture, drag the side or corner handles. You can see how near the kangaroos are currently in the picture below.

+ Click the "Commit" button (a blue check mark) whenever you're satisfied with your creation. Remember that you may need to slightly retouch the seam. As you can see in the picture, the horizon line is not quite aligned. Use the Clone Stamp or the Healing Brush to repair the seam.

Using One-Step Auto Repairs

The automatic lighting, contrast, and color correction capabilities in Elements may improve the appearance of your photos with a single menu command. These commands may be used in Quick mode or Advanced mode. The Enhance menu has them all.

Auto Smart Repair

The Auto Smart Fix tool may change anything, as its name suggests. The purpose of this tool is to correct color balance and emphasize features in regions that are dark. The too bright red-and-green picture on the left was much improved using the Auto Smart Fix command.

If the Auto Smart Fix was too "auto" for you, you may attempt Adjust Smart Fix, which is a step up. Similar to Auto Smart Fix, this function allows you to adjust the amount of picture correction via a slider that you, not Elements, may use.

Auto-Smart Tone

The purpose of the Auto Smart Tone auto fix is to alter the tonal values of the picture.
Take these actions to make this adjustment:
- Choose Enhance > Auto Smart Tone in Advanced or Quick mode while your picture is open. Elements automatically make a default correction.
- The "joystick" (the two-circle symbol in the center of the picture) may be moved to adjust your adjustment. By glancing at the thumbnail previews in each corner, you can see how the picture will appear as you move the joystick in that direction. You may see pictures of the changes done before and after by moving the Before and After switch.
- Click the Learn from This Correction option (arrow with lines icon) in the dialog box's lower left corner. Elements will "learn" from this editing session as a result.

Upon choosing this option, Elements records the adjustments you made to this picture and use those modifications to decide where to position the joystick on the subsequent image you open and modify. As more photos are corrected, Auto Smart Tone adjustments improve over time.

This clever algorithm can distinguish between several picture kinds based on the appearance of the tones and determine which modification is most effective for each type. It's possible that your changes are disrupting the learning archive. Select Edit > Preferences > General > Reset AutoSmart Tone Learning (or Adobe Photoshop Elements Editor > Preferences > General > Reset Auto Smart Tone Learning if you're on a Mac) to reset it.

- Once you are satisfied with the modification, you may click OK. To begin over, click the "Reset" button.

Automatic Levels

The Auto Levels command modifies the overall contrast of a picture. The picture should already have a fair amount of contrast, meaning that the shadow, highlight, and midtone regions all have the same range of tones and detail, for this command to function as best it can. Auto Levels converts your image's brightest and darkest pixels to black and white. As a result, the shadows seem deeper and the highlights appear brighter.

Although the Auto Levels option might improve contrast, it may also introduce an unwanted color cast. Undo the operation and use the Auto Contrast command instead to resolve this. If it doesn't improve the situation, it's time to use the heavy weapons.

Auto Contrast

You may alter an image's overall contrast without altering its color by using the Auto Contrast command. This command maintains the image's color balance better than the Auto Levels command, but it may not enhance contrast as well. Using Auto Contrast reduces the likelihood of the strange color casts that sometimes occur while using Auto Levels. This command works well on hazy images.

Removal of Auto Haze

As you can see here, the Auto Haze Removal command does a much better job of eliminating haze in photos than the Auto Contrast function. Additionally, be sure to examine the Enhance menu's Haze Removal command, which is accessible in both Advanced and Quick modes. You may press a few more alternatives to improve the clarity of your photograph when you click on that instruction.

Automatic Color Correction

By focusing on the picture's highlights, midtones, and shadows rather than its color channels, the Auto Color Correction command modifies the color and contrast of an image. It then modifies the values of the white and black pixels and balances out the midtones. The illustration below demonstrates how to utilize this arrangement to remove a color cast or level out the colors in your image. In some cases, this remark may also be helpful in correcting oversaturated or undersaturated colors.

Automatic Sharpening

Digitally captured images or flatbed scanned images often lack sufficient detail. Sharpening gives the impression that the picture is more focused by increasing the contrast between pixels. Auto Sharpen makes an effort to improve focus without going overboard. What happens if excessive sharpening is done? Your formerly smooth visual quality suddenly becomes loud and rough. Make sharpness the final thing you perform after you're done with all the other repair and enhancement jobs.

Auto Red-Eye Fix

It's simple to comprehend what the Auto Red Eye Fix command accomplishes. It automatically identifies and corrects red eyes in a picture. A human or animal's eyes become crimson when they stare directly at the flash. In addition, the red eye may be blue, green, or yellow. If the Auto Red Eye Fix doesn't help, you may always utilize the Red Eye tool in the Tools panel.

Here's how to manually get rid of red eyes:

- Select the Red Eye Removal tool from the Tools menu. Another option is to hit Y.
- Click the red part of your image's eye using the preset settings. With a single click, this tool darkens the pupil while maintaining the overall tone and shape of the eye. Repeat with the opposite eye.
- **You may alter one or both of these parameters in the Tool Options if you don't like the fix:**
  - **Pupil Radius:** You may adjust the pupil's size with the pupil radius slider.
  - **Darken:** You may adjust the pupil's darkness or lightness using the slider.

Remember that photos in which the subject has closed their eyes may also be corrected. You'll need another picture of them with their eyes open. If that source picture is not accessible, you will need to provide another one. Pets might have white, green, blue, or yellow eyes thanks to the light. One option in Elements' Tool Options is "Pet Eye." If this option doesn't work, the Color Replacement tool is the best option to attempt.

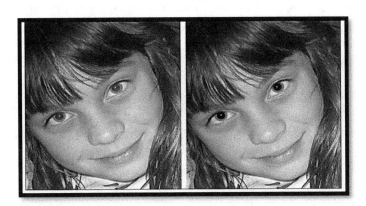

Quick Mode Editing

- After selecting the Editor Button at the workspace's bottom, choose the Quick button at the top. After choosing one or more images in the Organizer, this is what happens. Alternately, if you're in Advanced mode, click the Quick button at the top of the workspace after choosing the desired picture or images from the Photo Bin.

Note: By selecting the desired file and pressing the Open button, you may also open photos.

- To choose your preferred preview, use the View drop-down list located at the top of the workspace. In either vertical or horizontal orientation, you may examine your original picture (Before only), your fixed image (After only), or both images side by side (Before & After).

- The Zoom and Hand tools allow you to move around and enlarge your picture. Use the Zoom tool to click on a picture to see it up close. Press Alt (Option on a Mac) to zoom out. Drag the image within the image window to move it around. To adjust the Zoom percentage, you may also utilize the Zoom slider located in the top right corner of the workspace or in the Tool Options.
- To choose the desired window view, click one of the options in the Tool Options: Fit Screen, fit Screen (which enlarges the picture to fit the screen), 1:1 (Actual Pixels), or Print Size. Another Zoom slider is included in the Tool Options.
- To crop your picture, use the Crop tool located in the Tools panel.
- Click the Rotate Left or Rotate Right buttons in the Options panel located at the bottom left of the workspace to rotate the picture by 90 degrees. You may access the Rotate Right button by clicking the arrow adjacent to Rotate Left.
- To make any required corrections, use Auto Contrast, Auto Color Correction, Auto Levels, Auto Smart Fix, and others.

These instructions are all located under Smart Fix, Lighting, and Color in the Enhance menu or the Adjustments pane of the workspace. To see the instructions, click the Adjustments button located in the workspace's lower right corner. Remember that one fix is often sufficient. Avoid stacking them on top of one another. If the first one doesn't work, try another one by clicking the "Reset" button in the top right corner of the picture preview. If you are not satisfied with the outcome, you should go to step 8. If you're all right, you may go on to Step 9.

- To have additional control over Smart Fix, Exposure, Lighting, Color, and Balance, utilize the sliders or click on the thumbnails in the Adjustments panel on the right side of the screen if the auto repairs aren't sufficient. You may watch a live preview of each modification by moving your mouse pointer over any of the thumbnails in the window.

The slider automatically adjusts to correspond. **The following is a synopsis of each modification that may be made using the drop-down choices for Exposure, Lighting, Color, and Balance:**

➢ **Exposure:** Modifies the brightness or darkness of a picture. To make it brighter or darker, adjust the slider from left to right. The values range from –4 to 4 and are expressed in f-stop increments.

➢ **Shadows:** Without changing the highlights, moving the slider to the right lightens the darkest areas of your picture.

➢ **Midtones:** Modifies the middle grayscale values' intensity. Doesn't alter the shadows or highlights.

➢ **Highlights:** Your image's brighter areas darken as you move the slider to the right, but the shadows remain the same.

➢ **Saturation:** Modifies the colors' brightness.

➢ **Hue:** Modifies every hue in a picture. Make a choice initially if you want to alter only a few components' colors. Otherwise, make this modification with caution.

➢ **Vibrance:** Modifies the intensity of a picture by intensifying less saturated colors relative to more saturated ones. This option aims to minimize clipping (or color loss) by raising saturation while maintaining the same skin tones. Slide the slider to the right to increase the saturation.

➢ **Temperature:** By adjusting the temperature, the colors become either paler (blue) or warmer (red). Photographs that are too warm, too chilly (such as those shot in the winter with snow), or skin tones may all be corrected with this change.

➢ **Tint:** You may change the tint after adjusting the temperature to make the hue more purple or green. Additionally, you may choose which parts of your photograph need corrections. Quick Mode provides the Quick selecting tool for your selecting chores.

➥ To add final adjustments, use the additional tools in the Tools menu. **The functions of each tool are listed below:**

➢ **Red Eye Removal Tool:** To eliminate red eyes in humans, use the Auto Red Eye Fix. Try the Red Eye tool if that doesn't work.

➢ **Whiten Teeth:** As the name suggests, this remedy whitens your teeth. Make sure you use the Tool Options' Size slider to choose the appropriate brush size. By selecting the Brush Settings button, you may adjust the brush tip's Hardness, Spacing, Roundness, and Angle. Your lips chin, and other places will be whitened if you use a brush whose diameter is more than your teeth. Press the teeth together. Note: This tool simultaneously selects and whitens. Following the first click, the Tool Options selection option changes from "New Selection" to "Add to Selection." To eliminate excess items from your dental selection, click the "Subtract from Selection" button and then click the desired location. After teeth whitening, if you are satisfied with the appearance of your teeth, pick pick → Deselect or tap Ctrl+D ((⌘+D on a Mac).

> ➤ **Spot Healing Brush/Healing Brush:** These instruments are excellent for repairing defects of all sizes (Spot Healing Brush vs. Healing Brush).
- (Optional) Click on your picture with the Text tool and add whatever text you wish. To fine-tune where your text is positioned, utilize the Move tool in Quick mode.
- To have the picture sharpened automatically, click the Auto button under Sharpen in the right pane.

Another option is to choose Enhance and then Auto Sharpen. If automated sharpening isn't working, you may manually change the Sharpen slider. The Quick mode has additional panels. Click the Effects icon in the workspace's lower right corner to access various effects. By choosing the Classic option, you may apply effects to your picture, like Toy Camera and Cross Process. You may add borders, such as the Scrapbook and Comic ones, to the corners of your image by clicking the Frames button. Additionally, you may access textures like Sunburst and Cracked Paint by clicking on the Textures button. You may click the Adjustments button to return to this panel's default settings. Click on the thumbnail in the pane you want to use to utilize any frame, material, effect, or effect.

Using Tools to Correct Minor Flaws

You may correct minor flaws in your photos with the help of elements. The Clone Stamp tool allows you to clone portions of a picture. Blemishes may be fixed using the Healing Brush and Spot Healing Brush tools. Small areas may be made lighter or darker using the Dodge and Burn tools. The focus may be altered using the Blur and Sharpen tools. Color may be fixed using the Sponge and Color Replacement tools.

Using the Clone Stamp tool for cloning

Elements allow you to clone elements without the hassle of genetically modifying DNA. Only pixels are copied from one location to another using the Clone Stamp tool. Cloning is a more realistic way to preserve soft-edged components, such as shadows, than selecting and then copying and pasting.

The Clone Stamp tool may still do effective repairs in many situations, even if it has been partly displaced from the retouching field by the introduction of the healing tools (covered in the sections that follow).

Use the Clone Stamp tool by doing the following:

- Select the Clone Stamp tool from the Tools panel in Advanced mode. It resembles a real rubber stamp in analog form. If the Pattern Stamp tool was used most recently, choose the Clone Stamp tool from the Tool options.
- Select a brush from the Tool Options' Brush Preset Picker panel. After that, you can either use the brush exactly as is or adjust its size using the Size slider. Additionally, keep in mind that the brush size you select should match the object you wish to retouch or clone. When cloning a large object, use a large brush. Small imperfections can be fixed with a tiny brush. Generally speaking, cloning with a soft-edged brush produces more realistic results.
- Select the desired percentages for Opacity and Blend Mode. To make your cloned image appear ghosted, use an opacity percentage below 100%.
- The Aligned option can be selected or deselected. When you move the pointer to a new location when Aligned is selected, the clone source moves as well. If you want to clone more than once from the same location, do not use the Aligned option.
- The Sample All Layers check box may be selected or deselected. This option allows you to choose pixels for the clone from every visible layer. The Clone Stamp tool will only copy from the active layer if you uncheck this option.
- To make a layer visible, click the Clone Overlay button. Displaying an overlay might be useful when you need to ensure that the picture you're copying is aligned with the one below. Select the Check box for Show Overlay in the Clone Overlay dialog box. Change how transparent your layer is. When you choose Auto Hide, a ghosted preview of how your cloned pixels would look on the picture shows when you let go of the mouse. The overlay is hidden while you're copying, however. If you pick "Clipped," the overlay will only be within the lines of your brush. I feel this helps you clone what you want more accurately. Finally, pick Invert Overlay to invert the colors and tones of your overlay.
- Alt-click (Option-click on the Mac) the region of your picture that you wish to clone to designate the source of the clone.
- The location where you want the clone to appear may be selected by clicking or dragging. While you drag, Elements displays a crosshair cursor in addition to your Clone Stamp cursor. The Clone Stamp pointer indicates where the clone is being applied, and the crosshair indicates where you are cloning from. The crosshair travels with the mouse, giving you a constant reference to the portion of your picture that you're copying. If you don't pay attention, you can end up cloning something you don't want.
- Continue repeating Steps 7 and 8 until you have copied the desired portion. If you selected the Aligned option, try cloning an element without moving your mouse. When fixing a fault, you should also aim to avoid going overboard. It is typically sufficient to click on each defect one or two times. Overuse of the Clone Stamp will result in a blotchy appearance that indicates that something has been touched up.

Using the Healing Brush to Retouch

Similar to the Clone Stamp tool, the Healing Brush tool allows you to clone pixels from one area to another. However, the Healing Brush is superior because it analyzes the highlights, midtones, and blacks of the area to determine the problem. The Healing Brush will utilize the colors around the brush stroke and the pattern from the sampled region as its source if you paint over an imperfect area. The restoration is less blotchy and off-color than the Clone Stamp tool repair since the highlights, midtones, and shadows remain the same. **Take the following actions to repair a picture:**

- Open the picture that needs to be altered in Advanced mode, then choose the Healing Brush tool from the Tools panel. The instrument resembles a bandage. You may alternate between the Healing Brush and Spot Healing Brush tools by pressing the J key. You may also choose one of these tools and then go to the Tool Options and pick the other tool. Indeed, you may also recover in between two images. Simply ensure that they are both in the same color mode, such as RGB (red, green, and blue). I chose a few that may need some improvement but look fantastic in photos.

- Choose a size for the Healing brush tool in the Tool Options. The Hardness, Spacing, Angle, and Roundness may also be changed under the Brush Settings. Don't be timid. Be remembering to adjust the brush's size as necessary. To make the outcome appear true, you must use the proper brush size for the fault you're addressing.

- Pick the blend mode you desire. Most of the time, you should leave the setting as Normal while you're retouching. The borders of your lines will still exhibit film grain or noise when you employ Replace mode.

- **One of the following Source choices is available to you:** Sampled makes use of the image's pixels. For the majority of your repairs, you choose this option. Pattern uses pixels from a pattern selected from the Pattern Picker drop-down menu.

- The Aligned option may be selected or deselected. You should likely leave Aligned picked for most retouching work. The details of each choice are as follows:
  - ➤ **With Aligned selected:** Elements displays a crosshair next to the Healing Brush cursor when you click or drag with the Healing Brush. The crosshair indicates the sample point, also known as the source. You can always see the area you're sampling since the crosshair remains in the same spot when you move the Healing Brush tool.
  - ➤ **With Aligned deselected:** When Aligned is not selected, Elements will always utilize the source pixels from the initial sample point, regardless of how many times you pause and begin dragging.

- To use all of the visible layers to repair a picture, tick the Sample All Layers box. You can only heal from the active layer if you uncheck this option. On top of the picture you want to repair, create a fresh, blank layer by selecting the Sample All Layers box. Later on, you'll have the most edit possibilities if you do this. After the picture has been repaired, you may modify the opacity, blend modes, and other settings on the healed layer. This is because the pixels, rather than the actual picture, appear on the new layer.

- You may click the Clone Overlay option if you'd like.

- Alt-clicking will create the sample point (or Option-clicking on a Mac). Make sure you click on the area of the picture that you want to duplicate. I worked on each individual in this instance and clicked on a smooth facial feature.
- Click or drag over a problematic region of your picture after releasing the Alt (or Option on the Mac) key. You're healing from the crosshair, so pay attention to it. The forehead, jaw, and eye creases were wiped aside. This pair never looked better, and they had no recuperation time at all.

Using the Spot Healing Brush to focus

While the Spot Healing Brush corrects minor imperfections, the Healing Brush corrects larger ones. The only option that is compatible with both is Content-Aware, which we will discuss in Step 3 of the following steps. The Spot Healing Brush does not require you to select a sampling source. It immediately obtains a sample from the problematic area. It's easy, quick, and generally effective. However, since the sampling source cannot be changed, be on the lookout for subpar fixes. **Use the Spot Healing Brush tool to quickly correct defects by doing the following:**

- Open your picture in Advanced mode, then choose the Spot Healing Brush tool. The instrument has an oval form with dots on it, like a bandage. You may alternate between the Healing Brush and Spot Healing Brush tools by pressing the J key. You may also choose one of these tools and then go to the Tool Options and pick the other tool.
- Use the Brush Preset Picker in the Tool Options to choose a brush tip. By using the Size slider, you may further alter the diameter. Additionally, you may adjust the brush size by pressing the left and right brackets, respectively. Select a brush somewhat larger than the area you want to repair.
- **Select the kind from the Tools menu:**
  - ➢ Proximity Match: This kind fixes the damaged region by sampling the pixels around the selection's edge.
  - ➢ **Create Texture:** This kind corrects the error by using every pixel in the selection to create a texture.
  - ➢ **Content-Aware:** If you want to remove anything larger than a freckle or mole, this is the ideal option. The problem is fixed by using the actual content of the picture. You

can zap large items away. I got rid of the female on the swing, as you can see in the picture below. Note: To get the desired effect, you may need to paint over the item more than once. To remedy the issue, you may also need to utilize the Clone Stamp or other repair tools. First, attempt Proximity Match. If it doesn't work, undo it and try Content-Aware or Create Texture. If you wish to get rid of wider sections, you can also use Edit > Fill Selection and chose Content-Aware from the Use pop-up option.

- To use all of the visible layers to repair a picture, tick the Sample All Layers box. This check box must remain unchecked in order for you to recover from the current layer.
- To repair an area, click, drag, or "paint" over it. As you can see in the pictures below, I used the Spot Healing Brush to paint over the girl on the swing and get realistic effects.

If the Healing or Spot Healing Brushes don't seem to be helpful, you might try the Object Removal Guided Edit in Guided mode under Special Edits. Once you have chosen one of the four tools, use the Clone Stamp or Spot Healing Brush to address any remaining issues. Please note that you may only use this change if the item you want to remove doesn't impact anything you want to preserve.

Using the Content-Aware Move tool to reposition

The Content-Aware Move tool allows you to choose and move a portion of a picture. The fact that content-aware technology fills in the gap left by shifting that section is one of its strongest features. To put it another way, Elements fills in the gaps with relevant material after examining the region around the section you have selected to move.

Here's how to use this practical editing tool:

- Open your picture in Advanced mode, then choose the Content-Aware Move tool. The instrument resembles two arrows. Another option is to hit Q.
- **Select the Extend or Move mode.**
  - **Move:** After moving your selection, Elements fills in the empty area with content-aware pixels. When you need to relocate one or more elements in a photograph to

improve the composition, the relocate mode is excellent. Keep in mind that this technique works best when the object's current backdrop resembles the background it was borrowed from.

> **Extend:** Elements merge into the current item while extending the region you choose while retaining any lines or structural components. You may use this option to make things like hair, fur, trees, buildings, and larger or smaller. I moved the girl to the right using the Move mode to add some text to the picture below.

- Select your preferred healing environment. Elements' flexibility in moving pixels about and the content-aware fill's strictness in maintaining regions are both adjustable. I stayed with the default option, which is right in the center. You may also click the Sample All Layers option to utilize content from all of your layers. Only content from the current layer is used when this box is deselected.

- To move or expand a portion of your picture, drag it around. To fine-tune your choice, use the Path Operations tools located on the tools tab. To add anything to your selection on a Mac, click Shift; to remove something from it, press Option (or Alt for Windows). You may also alter the area's size or rotation by selecting the Transform on Drop option. When you move your selection, the morph box and transform choices will appear in the options bar. The handles of your morph box may be manually rotated or dragged there, or you can choose your alternatives. Click the "Commit" button, which resembles a blue checkmark, to complete the transition.

- Move your pick to the desired location if you did not choose the Transform on Drop option in Step 4. Deselect the option.

- Any places that need it should be touched up. Any errors or problems that remain may be fixed using the Healing or Clone Stamp tools. I adjusted a few spots on the girl that weren't quite in alignment. Spot-healing was also done on the unsightly light fixture at the top of the picture.

Additionally, a Content-Aware choice may be filled in at any selected location. Select anything to fill in, then click "Edit." The Use pop-up menu will show up under Contents. Click on the list and choose Content-Aware.

Using Dodge and Burn tools to lighten and darken

The first applications of dodging and burning were in the darkroom, when photographers added or removed exposure to fix negatives with an excessive number of dark or bright regions. They accomplished this by creating prints with holes and paddles. Because they are more precise and have more applications, the Dodge and Burn tools are superior to the conventional ones they replaced. By choosing from a variety of brush tips, you may customize the tool's size and softness. Furthermore, you can only adjust specific tonal ranges in your picture, like the highlights, midtones, and shadows. Finally, you may input an exposure percentage to modify the amount of correction applied. Use these tools sparingly and only on specific areas of your image, such as the girl's face in the image below. You can even choose before dodging and burning to ensure that the change only impacts your specific area. Additionally, keep in mind that you are unable to add previously unexisting information. When you attempt to lighten very dark, low-detail shadows, you end up with gray areas. White blobs are the result of attempting to darken highlights that are too light.

Do the following to avoid or burn an image:
- Select the Dodge or Burn tool from the Tools panel to lighten or darken in Advanced mode. These two tools resemble a darkroom paddle and an O-shaped hand, respectively. Press O to toggle between the Dodge and Burn tools. Furthermore, you have the option to pick any of these tools and then choose the desired tool from the Tool Options.
- From the Brush Preset Picker panel, choose a brush and, if required, change the brush's size. Larger, softer brushes spread the dodging or burning effect over a larger area, making it easier to mix with the background.
- Select Highlights, Midtones, or Shadows from the Range drop-down menu. To brighten or darken the darkest portions of your picture, choose Shadows. Select Midtones to alter the typical darkness tones. To alter how light or dark the spots are, select Highlights. I avoided the shadows because the image above used to have a lot of dark spots.

- By modifying the Exposure setting in the Tool Options, you can decide how much correction you wish to apply with each stroke. Starting with a smaller percentage gives you more control over how much is lightened or darkened. Exposure can be used in the same manner as the standard Brush tool's opacity setting. The setting I used was 10%.
- Paint over the areas you want to lighten or darken. If you don't like the results, press Ctrl+Z (⌘ +Z on the Mac) to undo.

Smudging away rough spots

When you start to drag with the Smudge tool, one of the focus tools, the color under the cursor moves your pixels around. Picture pulling a brush through wet paint. You can make different effects with this tool. When used too much, it can make the result look strange. You can soften the edges of objects in a more natural way than you can with the Blur tool when you use it more subtly, though. Alternatively, you can produce pictures that look like paintings. However, keep an eye on your image as you work because if you're not careful with the Smudge tool, you can start to lose details and mess things up.

Here's how to use the Smudge tool:

- Select the Smudge tool from the Tools panel while in Advanced mode. The tool looks like a finger. To switch between the Smudge, Blur, and Sharpen tools, press R. Furthermore, you have the option to pick any of these tools and then choose the desired tool from the Tool Options.

- From the Brush Preset Picker panel, choose a brush. You can fine-tune the size of your brush by moving the Size slider. To smudge small areas, like edges, use a small brush. The effects are extreme when you use bigger brushes.
- From the Mode drop-down menu, pick a blending mode.
- To choose how strong the smudging effect is, use the Strength slider or text box. The effect is lighter as the value goes down.

- Step 5 can be skipped if your image lacks layers. To make Elements use pixels from all the visible layers when creating the effect, select the Sample All Layers check box if your image has more than one layer. Only the active layer still has the smudge, but the way it looks changes based on the colors of the layers below it.
- Use the Finger-Painting option to begin the smudge by using the foreground color. In this case, the color under your cursor is not used. Instead, the foreground color is smeared at the start of each stroke. You can quickly go into Finger Painting mode if you want the best of both worlds. Hold down the Alt (or Option) key while you drag. To return to Normal mode, release Alt (or Option on a Mac).
- Paint over the areas you want to smudge. Pay close attention to your strokes, because this tool can make big changes to your images. It's easy to cancel the changes by pressing Ctrl+Z (or cmd+Z on a Mac). Then, lower the Strength percentage even more.

Blur tool for softening

In addition to repairing pictures, the Blur tool (which resembles a teardrop) can be used for more creative projects. The Blur tool can smooth out a small flaw or part of a rough edge. You can give something a little blur to make it look like it was moving when it was shot. Sometimes blurring parts of an image can help draw attention to the main subject, like in the image below where I blurred everything but the girl's face. The Blur tool blurs an area by making the pixels next to each other less contrasty.

The mechanics of using the Blur tool and its options are similar to those of the Smudge tool. When you use the Blur tool, be sure to use a small brush for smaller areas of blur.

On and off splashing color

The Sponge tool either soaks up color or squeezes it out. More specifically, this tool changes the saturation, or intensity, of colors in both color and grayscale pictures. Yes, the Sponge tool can also be used in Grayscale mode. It does this by changing the color of the pixels to make them darker or lighter. You can use the Sponge tool to reduce or increase the saturation of chosen areas to draw attention to or away from them, just like you can with the Blur and Sharpen tools.

To sponge color on or off of your image, do these things:

- In Advanced mode, choose the Sponge tool from the Tools panel. The tool looks like a sponge. To switch between the Sponge, Dodge, and Burn tools, press O. Furthermore, you have the option to pick any of these tools and then choose the desired tool from the Tool Options.
- From the Brush Preset Picker panel, choose a brush. If you need to, you can adjust the brush tip even more. Use large, soft brushes to saturate or desaturate a larger area.
- From the Mode drop-down menu, choose either Desaturate or Saturate to decrease or increase the color intensity.
- Use the Flow slider or text box to pick a flow rate. The flow rate tells you how fast the effect of saturation or desaturation comes up as you paint. Start with a lower rate and make changes as needed.
- Paint carefully over the areas you want to saturate or desaturate with color. I used saturation to make the dog the main focus of the image below while desaturating the people.

Changing the hue of one thing to another

With the Color Replacement tool, you can change an image's foreground color to its original color. This tool can be used in many ways, such as:

- To give the appearance of a hand-painted photograph, colorize a grayscale image.
- The image below shows how I used the Color Replacement tool to paint part of the background black. This will completely change the color of an element or elements in your image.
- Get rid of red eyes (or yellow, green, or any other color in animals) if you're not happy with other, more automatic ways to do it.

One thing I like about the Color Replacement tool is that it keeps all of the image's tones. The color that is put on is not the same as the solid paint that is put on with the Brush tool. The midtones, shadows, and highlights stay the same when you are replacing the color. To use the Color Replacement tool, you must first take a sample of the image's original colors. Then, you must replace those colors with the foreground color. You can control the range of colors that Elements replaces by setting different sample methods, limits, and Tolerance. **To replace an existing color to your foreground color, do these things:**

- Select the Tools panel's Color Replacement tool in Advanced mode. The tool looks like a paintbrush with a small blue square next to it. To switch between the Brush, Impressionist Brush, and Color Replacement tools, press B. Furthermore, you have the option to pick any of these tools and then choose the desired tool from the Tool Options.
- In the Tool Options, go to the Brush Preset Picker panel and pick the brush tip you want. Adjust the size of your brush even more if you need to. Then, go to Brush Settings and change the hardness, spacing, roundness, and angle.
- Pick the blending mode you want. **Here is a quick list of each one:**
  - **Color:** This is the default mode, and it works well for most tasks. It will change the color but not the brightness, so your tonal range will stay the same. This mode is great for getting rid of red eyes.
  - **Hue:** This mode is similar to color, but it's not as intense and has a softer effect.
  - **Saturation:** This mode is the one to use to convert the color in your image to grayscale. Set your foreground color to Black on the Tools panel.
  - **Luminosity:** This mode, which is the opposite of Color, doesn't do much. No matter what color it is, it changes the brightness levels.
- **Pick the Limits mode you want. You can choose from these options:**
  - Contiguous replaces the color of pixels next to each other that have the sampled color.

- ➢ Discontiguous replaces the color of the pixels containing the sampled color, whether or not they're adjacent.
- ✦ Set your Tolerance percentage. Tolerance refers to a range of colors. The higher the value, the broader the range of color that's sampled, and vice versa.
- ✦ **Choose your Sampling method. You can choose from these options:**
  - ➢ Continuous allows you sample and change colors all the time as you move your cursor.
  - ➢ Once replaces color only where the first color you sample is present.
  - ➢ Background Swatch only replaces colors in places where your current Background color is present.
- ✦ Choose the Anti-aliasing option. Anti-aliasing makes the edges of the sampled areas a little smoother.
- ✦ Click or drag your picture. The foreground color substitutes the sampled regions' original colors.

CHAPTER SEVEN

NEW FEATURES AND AI-POWERED TOOLS

An overview of Photoshop Elements' AI with Adobe Sensei

Adobe's machine learning and artificial intelligence (AI) technology is called Adobe Sensei. Many of its products, like as Photoshop Elements, come with it. Its primary functions are to simplify difficult activities, automate tedious procedures, and provide insightful recommendations in order to increase user creativity and productivity. Users of Photoshop Elements may easily create sophisticated adjustments and effects using Adobe Sensei. Because of this, amateurs and casual users who may not know how to manually edit photographs might benefit from it.

Adobe Sensei-Powered Photoshop Elements' Principal Features

- **Auto Creations:** Adobe Sensei analyzes the photographs you've uploaded to produce Auto Creations, including as slideshows, photo collages, and effects like "photo remixes" or "dynamic slideshows." You may alter these artistic outputs or utilize them exactly as is. For those who don't want to spend time doing intricate modifications by hand but yet want fast results that appear professional, this tool is fantastic.

- **Auto Tagging and Organizing:** Adobe Sensei automatically assigns smart tags to your photos in the Elements Organizer depending on their subject matter. It can identify, for instance, dogs, mountains, beaches, and other items. Large picture collections are simpler to browse through and arrange as a result. To make organizing even simpler, Adobe Sensei-powered face recognition can also automatically group images of the same individual together.

- **Object Selection and Removal:** Some of the simplest tools are those for object selection and removal. With a single click, users can swiftly choose a person or item in a picture thanks to Sensei's AI, which intelligently detects edges to make decisions quicker and more accurate than when done by hand. The Remove Object tool can swiftly eliminate unnecessary objects from an image and fill in the gaps with pixels from the surrounding area to produce a smooth alteration. This is particularly helpful for removing items that detract from or detract from the scene.

- **Auto Colorization:** Adding color to black-and-white images is a breeze using Adobe Sensei's Auto Colorization tool. By examining the image, Sensei selects the appropriate hues for skin tones, attire, and organic components like grass and the sky. Although users may manually alter the results, the AI does the majority of the job automatically and creates accurate colorization with no effort.

- Adobe Sensei can identify the most crucial elements of a picture, such as the primary topic, and use Smart Selection to generate choices for you. This is particularly useful since it allows you to modify only the topic and leave the backdrop unaltered. Sensei expedites difficult work and ensures their timely and accurate completion.

- **Depth of Field and Blur Effects:** By adjusting or adding blur to highlight the background and center, the AI may create the illusion of depth of field. With the Depth Blur feature, users may choose a focus point, and the AI will apply a realistic depth effect to make the picture seem as if it was captured with a professional camera.
- **Skin Smoothing and Retouching:** Adobe Sensei assists in portrait retouching by automatically identifying and smoothing skin textures, eliminating imperfections, and enhancing the prominence of facial features. The AI intelligently softens the skin while preserving vital features like eyes and hair.
- **AI-Enhanced Guided Edits:** Adobe Sensei enhances a lot of Photoshop Elements' Guided Edits. Guided Edits walk you through complex tasks step-by-step, and Sensei's AI often intervenes to automate or provide improvements as you go. This covers tasks including mixing several images, applying effects, and creating intricate cuts and selections.

Adobe Sensei's Advantages for Users of Photoshop Elements

- **Usability:** With its AI-powered capabilities, Photoshop Elements is simple to use for users of all skill levels. Complex picture editing tasks may now be completed with a few clicks and don't need much knowledge.
- **Time-saving:** By automating time-consuming or repetitive operations like object removal, labeling, and photo organizing, Sensei frees up users' time so they can concentrate on more creative pursuits.
- **Professional Results for Novices:** Even those with little editing expertise may achieve professional results with the aid of AI-enhanced tools. Everyone may utilize Sensei's sophisticated tools to edit images, regardless of experience level.

Making use of the AI-driven Remove Tool

The AI-powered Remove Tool, one of Adobe Photoshop Elements 2025's most noteworthy features, makes it simpler to eliminate any extraneous items from your images. This application, which is powered by Adobe's AI, makes a labor-intensive task almost effortless. Using machine learning, the program automatically analyzes your picture, locates the item you want to remove, and seamlessly re-inserts it. Whether you want to eliminate distracting objects from landscapes or remove individuals from your vacation images, the Remove Tool can make the process fast and simple.

First Step: Choosing the Remove Tool

Start by locating the Remove Tool in the Photoshop Elements menu. Usually, a brush icon with a negative symbol next to it indicates it. If you are having problems locating it, you may use the search bar in Photoshop Elements or search in the menu on the left under the healing and retouching tools.

After choosing the Remove Tool, a number of alternatives will show up in the alternatives Bar at the top of the workspace. These settings allow you to customize the tool to suit the item you want to discard. Among other things, you may alter the brush's size, hardness, and feathering. The way the tool interacts with the picture will be altered by these modifications.

Second Step: Modifying the Size of the Brush

Before brushing over anything, it's crucial to adjust the brush size to suit the item you want to remove. You may adjust the brush's size using the slider in the Options Bar. A lower brush size will enable you to get more accurate results while altering tiny or complex objects. Higher objects, such as backdrops or buildings, may need a higher brush size in order to cover more land with fewer strokes.

The brush's hardness, which determines how soft or harsh the edges are, may also be changed. Softer edges make the deleted item blend in with the rest of the image when the backdrop is complex, such as with grass or water.

Third Step: Scrubbing the Surface

Now that the brush size has been established, all you need to do is brush over the item you want to remove. The tool immediately detects the boundaries of the item as you move the brush over it, then uses the surrounding pixels to fill in the empty area left by the deleted portion. For example, if you wish to remove light from a landscape image, the tool will use the surrounding trees and sky to fill in the gaps with complementary colors and textures. In real time, the AI determines the optimum way to replace the item, ensuring that the new material blends in with the surroundings to create a realistic appearance.

Fourth Step: Editing and Fine-Tuning

The initial removal may not have been flawless, particularly in images with intricate backgrounds. If that occurs, you may continue to refine the edit by brushing over the affected region. If you can still see bits of the item or if the region seems uneven, you may either adjust the settings or fine-tune your brush strokes to create a cleaner outcome. To ensure that the sand or water is smooth, you may need to go over the area many times if you're escorting someone off of a crowded beach. The Remove Tool may be used repeatedly without compromising the picture quality since Photoshop Elements employs a non-destructive editing technique. You may also utilize the Clone Stamp Tool to correct any little errors that the AI might have overlooked, or you can undo or redo modifications.

How to Achieve the Best Outcomes

- Use numerous passes for complicated items or backdrops. To thoroughly examine the region and make adjustments, the AI may need to apply a few brushstrokes.
- When dealing with situations that have a lot of diverse textures, such as grass, water, or the sky, feather the brush's edges to create seamless transitions.

- To work on minor details, zoom in. You have better control over the brushstrokes and can ensure that minor details like hair or garment borders are accurately eliminated when you zoom in.
- Play with opacity: If the removal seems too severe, reducing the brush's opacity might make the region blend in more subtly.

Dealing with Auto Creations

The Adobe Photoshop Elements or Adobe Premiere Elements Home screen will display a number of Auto Creations, or automatically produced pieces. Make use of Auto Creations' photo effects, such as Depth of Field, Painterly, and B&W Selection. Additionally, you may use video montages, image collages, and slideshows to highlight significant moments in your life. To modify the Auto Creations and save your modifications, you may use Adobe Photoshop Elements or Adobe Premiere Elements. The Auto Creation may also be immediately shared on other social media platforms.

Examine Auto Creations

Every time you launch Adobe Photoshop Elements or Adobe Premiere Elements, you may access the Home screen. Under the "Auto Creations" area of this page, you may see automatically created photo effects, including the Painterly and B&W choices. Using the number icons that show up under each image, you may go through the first five Auto Creations and combine images and videos to create collages, slideshows, and "Candid Moments." Select see All from the drop-down menu to see the complete list of Auto Creations in Elements. You may take the Auto Creation out of the list by clicking the " " in the lower left corner of the picture that contains it. Elements may create items specifically for you using your names, words, record titles, events, locations, persons, and local information. The images and videos you bring in are used to create these items.

Take note: You may be able to access Auto Creations if you have the appropriate tool open. You may still view image effects, photo layouts, and video effects if that's all you have on your computer. You can only watch video collages, slideshows, and candid moments using Adobe Premiere Elements. **All of the Auto Creations I have discussed so far will be visible to those who have both Adobe Photoshop Elements and Adobe Premiere Elements.**

- You won't be able to view the Home screen when you launch Adobe Photoshop Elements or Adobe Premiere Elements using a trick.
- You may get a preview of your Auto Creations on the Home screen. Before you can view it, you must choose Auto Creation.
- Before using Elements Organizer for the first time, you must upload images and videos and launch the application. As you upload more content, they will appear more often on your Home screen.
- Your previous Auto Creations will eventually be deleted if you don't edit or save them.
- Projects that employ videos, such as Candid Moments or video slideshows, are incompatible with the Adobe Photoshop Elements version that is available via the Windows App Store.
- You may have a peek at Auto Creations. These may be seen in the Depth of Field effect, the Painterly effect, the Pattern Brush effect, and the Black and White Selection effect.

Launch an Auto Creation

Auto Creations allows you to modify, save, and share your creation. Click the "Auto Creations" button on the Home screen. You will arrive to Auto Creations as a result. Click the "Open" button after selecting the selected Auto Creation to open it in the included Elements software. You may modify the Auto Creation type in Adobe Premiere Elements, Photoshop Elements, or Elements Organizer. You may open a picture collage or photo effects in Adobe Photoshop Elements. You may open a Candid Moment or a video collage in Adobe Premiere Elements. Elements Organizer allows you to see slide shows.

Modify an Auto-Creation

Once you open an Auto Creation, you may modify it. Depending on the kind of Auto Creation you created, you may be able to modify it in Photoshop Elements, Elements Organizer, or Adobe Premiere Elements. Photoshop Elements allows you to open a picture effect, including Depth of Field, Painterly, Pattern Brush, or B&W Selection. The application will launch the effect in the previous mode that was utilized, which may be Advanced or Quick mode. Go to Advanced mode and choose the Layers panel and menu to improve or personalize the effect. To modify the mask, go to the Layers panel. Click the Layer mask thumbnail after selecting the lock symbol on the layer containing the mask thumbnail in order to alter the mask. The Painterly effect will be altered as a result.

- Keep layers hidden. (Click on to make that layer invisible.)
- To adjust the brush's level of opacity, use the "Opacity" slider.

Preserve an Automatic Creation

After opening and editing the work, you will be able to save it. To save an Auto Creation, follow these steps:

- Select the "Save" option from the menu to save the photo effect or image collage you created in Photoshop Elements. Alternatively, you may select "File" and then "Save As." By default, all of your Auto Creations will be stored under "My Pictures."
- To save a video collage or candid moments, choose File > Save in Adobe Premiere Elements. To save a slideshow in Elements Organizer, choose Slideshow > Save and press the button in the top right corner.

Share your Auto Creation as soon as possible

You have the option to share your Auto Creation on any of your preferred social media platforms when you've finished tweaking it in Photoshop Elements.

- Click the Share button in the upper right corner of the Editor window for Photoshop Elements to display an Auto Creation to others. Select your preferred sharing method from the drop-down menu.
- After you've finished editing your Auto Creation in Adobe Premiere Elements, you may post it to all of your social network profiles.

You may upload it on a variety of platforms, including YouTube, Flickr, and Twitter. Click the Share button on the desktop and choose the appropriate option from the drop-down menu that displays to share an Auto-creation in Elements Organizer.

Auto-Generating Collages and Slideshows

The built-in features in Adobe Photoshop Elements make it simple to create collages and presentations. Thanks to the software's automatic and adjustable capabilities, you can easily transform your images into visually attractive presentations and artwork. This comprehensive tutorial explains how to use Photoshop Elements to create collages and presentations.

Generating a Slideshow

- **Launch the planner:** To choose the images you want to include in your slideshow, open the Organizer and browse through your collections.
  - ➢ To do this, go to the Organizer in Photoshop Elements. All of the images you have imported will be shown there.
  - ➢ Use the selection tool to choose the photographs for your slideshow (you may choose several images by holding down the Shift or Ctrl key).
- **Make Your Presentation:** After choosing your photographs, pick the Create option located in the Organizer's top right corner. After clicking this button, a choice of creative project possibilities will appear; choose Slideshow.
- **Personalization and Auto-Creation:** The auto-creation option allows Photoshop Elements to create a slideshow using the images you choose.
  - ➢ **Themes:** To alter the slideshow's look and motion effects, you may use a few pre-made themes.
  - ➢ **Music:** You may upload your own audio files or use one of Photoshop Elements' preset audio tracks to add background music.
  - ➢ **Text:** You may add titles, descriptions, or captions to your slideshow by using the Text Tool. This is helpful for adding dates, narrating a tale, or providing context to the images.
  - ➢ **Timing and Transitions:** To make the slideshow simpler and more engaging, you may choose from a variety of transition effects and alter the duration of each image.
- **Examine and Distribute:** Before saving your slideshow, you may see it in Preview from start to finish. You may ensure that everything is configured the way you like in this method. You may still alter the music, the time, or the picture sequence. Once you're satisfied, you may distribute the slideshow elsewhere:
  - ➢ **Sharing Options:** You may email or send it as a video file to friends, store it to your computer, or post it on social media.
  - ➢ **Burn to Disc:** In Photoshop Elements, you can also burn your slideshow to a DVD so that DVD players can play it.

Constructing a Collage

- **Launch the organizer:** As with the slideshow, begin by choosing the images you want to include in your collage using the Organizer. These might be a collection of linked event photographs or simply pictures you wish to artistically combine.
- **Make Your Collage of Photos:** After choosing the images you want to use, click the Create button in the Organizer's top right corner, and from the menu that displays, choose Photo Collage.
- **Customization of Layout and Auto-Creation:** Using the images you choose, Photoshop Elements will automatically generate a collage arrangement. The photographs are

arranged in a grid or another pre-made template by the application. The layout may be easily altered by:

> **Rearranging Photos:** Drag and drop the images to rearrange their placement inside the collage.
> **Adding Text:** To personalize your collage, you may alter the type, color, size, and alignment of text components such as quotations, captions, or event details with the Text Tool.
> **Effects and Filters:** You may use effects or filters to highlight certain images in the collage. To give your collage a distinctive appearance, you may, for instance, apply vintage effects, convert certain images to black and white, or apply creative filters.

- **Conserve and Distribute:** Once your collage is complete, there are many methods to save and share it:
  > **Print the Collage:** In Photoshop Elements, you can export your collage as a high-resolution picture that is prepared for printing. You have the option of having a professional print it or doing it yourself.
  > **Export for Web or Social Media:** The collage may also be exported for online usage, such as when it's included in a blog post or shared on social media.

Some Advice for Improving Your Projects

- **Consistency:** Keeping your theme or style consistent gives your collages or presentations a polished, expert appearance. Make sure that every element you use, whether it is color schemes, typefaces, or filters, complements the tone or idea you're attempting to convey.
- **Try Different Layouts:** Photoshop Elements offers a variety of layout choices for collages, ranging from simple grids to intricate and creative configurations. To choose which design best suits your photos, try out a few different ones.

Automated Photo Organization and Curation

The "Auto Curate" feature has been added to Photoshop Elements' Organizer section. This program automatically examines and sorts your images using AI-driven algorithms based on many criteria, including topic focus, faces, and picture quality. Users may more easily search through enormous collections of pictures and work with the best or most relevant images thanks to the Auto Curate tool, which automatically selects the best photos or photos that fit certain criteria. **The Auto Curate feature in Photoshop Elements may function as follows:**

- **Image Analysis:** Photoshop Elements analyzes several aspects of your images, including quality, faces, lighting, layout, and topic emphasis, using artificial intelligence and machine learning.
- **Automatic Selection:** Images are chosen and categorized into several categories or tiers by the Auto Curate tool using the analysis. For instance, it may identify and present pictures with the greatest focus, design, or recognizable faces.

- **Sorting and Grouping:** These photos are then sorted by the program into several groups or categories. This eliminates the need for users to manually search through the whole collection in order to locate and access photographs that fit certain criteria.
- User Control: By allowing or refusing to let the Auto Curate feature's ideas go wild, the user may sometimes alter the selection criteria or improve it.

The Organizer window's top right corner has the Auto Curate check box. Elements will examine the images in the Media Browser window without your intervention if you tick the option next to Auto Curate. After you're finished, the media browser will only display the finest images that Elements independently discovered.

Depth Blur: Using AI to provide depth-of-field effects

The new AI-powered Depth Blur filter will apply blur precisely where it's required once you choose your focus point. **To get the desired effect, you may then adjust the blur intensity, focus range, and focal distance.**

- **Choose the Depth Blur Tool:** To choose the Depth Blur tool, choose Neural Filters from the Filter menu.
- **Modify the Focal Range:** This indicates the region that is in focus. When concentrating on a particular topic, you may use the sliders to select whether to blur the backdrop.
- **Adjust Blur Strength:** The blur effect's intensity may be altered by adjusting the blur strength.
- **Fine-Tune Details:** To improve the overall effect, adjust parameters like haze, temperature, tint, saturation, brightness, and grain.

⊥ **Apply the Filter:** After you're satisfied with the settings, apply the filter to your picture. Without requiring a lot of manual adjustments, this tool makes it simple to achieve expert-looking depth-of-field effects.

Use the four new Quick Actions to create motion effects

The new Quick Actions panel is next to Effects while you're in Quick mode. You may instantly access 30 of the most well-liked one-click adjustments using it. Among other things, you may smooth skin, dehaze, colorize, blur or eliminate a backdrop, and more. To improve the outcome even more, you may click the Fine-tune option. Five new fast actions will be included in Photoshop Elements 2025. Four new "Add Motion" fast actions have been added, along with one dubbed "Depth Blur." These actions, which are based on Photoshop Elements' Moving photographs and Moving Overlays capabilities help to make your still photographs come to life by adding motion. The app now has a collection of music presets that you may choose from to add music to the Moving Overlays function.

To see how these features function, go to the Quick Actions panel in the Quick Workspace and choose the Add Motion area.

⊥ **Motion Blur:** This simulates movement by adding a dynamic blur effect. Ideal for action photos.

⊥ **Zoom Burst:** This function produces the appearance of a sudden burst in your photos by zooming in on a focus point.

⊥ **Spin Blur:** This function is excellent for creating the illusion that wheels and other round objects are moving since it produces a circular blur around a selected point.

⊥ **Route Blur:** Excellent for indicating the direction of motion, this feature creates a route for the blur to follow.

CHAPTER EIGHT
THE BEGINNER GUIDED EDITS

The Guided Edit mode offers a wide range of editing choices. Some are quite simple, like color correction, while others are far more complex, including tilt-shift, landscape stitching, and painting effects. In addition to being a useful tool, it offers inspiration for image editing. The following parts make up this fantastic editing room.

Fundamentals

If you want to get the most out of your digital images, you should apply this edit. By selecting Advanced > Enhance > Adjust Lighting > Brightness and Contrast, you may also locate this. **You may improve the image's appearance simply by increasing the contrast and brightness.**

- **Correct Skin Tone:** Removes color blemishes and marks. By selecting Advanced > Enhance > Adjust Color > Adjust Color for Skin Tone, you may also locate it.
- **Crop Photo:** To enhance an image's design, eliminate extraneous components.
- Levels are a powerful and user-friendly tool for modifying brightness and contrast. It serves a crucial purpose. Additionally, choose Advanced > Enhance > Levels > Adjust Lighting.
- I find that Levels perform better than the straightforward Lighten and Darken function.
- **Move and Scale item:** To effectively pick, copy, retouch, and paste an item, using the "Move and Scale Object" tool. This is a logical progression to the next function, Object Removal.
- Object Removal is an excellent function that enables you to immediately remove objects from an image. It makes use of the Healing Brush tool and Adobe AI. To get rid of anything you don't want, just draw a rough circle around it.
- **Resize Your Photo:** Changing the scale of any picture file may be done quickly and easily with this method.
- **Rotate and Straighten:** This is a basic tool for leveling pictures.
- **Sharpen:** This tool makes it simple to enhance the clarity of a picture, particularly if you want to print it.
- By using the vignette effect, you may highlight a main topic by darkening the image's edges.
- Color
- **Enhance Color:** This function uses the powerful Hue/Saturation tool to make colors seem better. Very important.
- **Lomo Camera Effect:** It gives photos a cool "look" by enhancing their contrast and blur. It looks nice.
- **Eliminate a Color Cast:** This is an effective method for improving the appearance of colors.

- **Saturated Film Effect:** Using this technique to highlight the colors is fast and simple. It functions nicely and is easy to use.

White and Black

Only color photographs may be converted to black and white with this capability. You may also use the service to convert the image to black and white on the Enhance page.

- As an added bonus, B&W Color Pop will preserve a color of your choosing. This and the previous one are identical. Produces high-quality graphical effects without requiring much expertise.
- **B&W Selection:** Just like the previous one, except you choose which color region to preserve. One or more colors might be included.
- **High Key:** Excellent, visual outcome.
- **Line Drawing:** The same as above, but it creates a special effect that resembles an image.
- **Low Key:** Images that are somber and dark look well in this setting.

About Fun edits

- **Double Exposure:** Combine two images to create a stylish 1960s style.
- Any picture may be transformed into a two-color masterpiece with a brand-new tool called the Duotone Effect. Although it has long existed in Photoshop CC, this latest edition makes it easier to use. It's excellent for creating unique styles with a single hue.
- A simple but powerful technique for breaking a picture up into "parts," such as a diptych (two panels) or triptych (three panels), and giving each one a unique visual impact is effects collage. Because everything is done for you, it's clever and simple to use.
- Making a cool image for Facebook or Instagram is easy with Meme Maker.
- **Multi-Photo Text:** This modification utilizes a distinct picture for each letter of the effect, much as Photo Text does. To fit into each letter in the design, a large number of various images must be prepared.
- **Old Fashioned picture:** This effect blends a graphic picture effect with some texture overlays and a "look" in sepia tones.
- Out of Bounds allows you to apply a fantastic 3D effect to certain areas of your images that are exclusive to those areas.
- **Painterly:** Painterly allows you to add the appearance of rough brushstrokes to any picture file. When printed on rough printer paper or watercolor paper, the picture looks fantastic.
- **Partial Sketch:** This feature converts the image to a one-color line drawing while allowing some of the original colors to show through the layer. These are excellent illustrations.
- You can now apply a visual design to the backdrop and, shockingly, behind the subject using a new tool called the Pattern Brush. This is due to the fact that it chooses the primary topic of the image itself. It functions effectively.

- **Photo Text:** You may use any image to fill text if you want a strong, graphic appearance. Styles that are really heavy, broad, bold, or extra-bold work well with it.
- **Picture Stack:** This function transforms any collection of images into a lovely stack of prints. This feature allows you to use AI to create a visually appealing product in a matter of seconds. It saves you time.
- **Pop Art:** Do you recall images of Marilyn Monroe and cereal boxes from the 1960s? This posterization and screen print resemble Andy Warhol's. Well done.
- **Puzzle Effect:** This technique divides a picture into pieces that resemble a jigsaw puzzle using a simple visual layer.
- **Reflection:** When you apply this effect, the top portion of the picture should seem to be reflecting in the bottom glass or water. Not every image can make advantage of it.
- **Shape Overlay Effect:** The Cookie Cutter tool allows you to create the entertaining Shape Overlay Effect. With this, you may turn your creations into scrapbooks.
- When employing the Speed Effect, a Motion Blur effect gives the picture a sensation of movement.
- To give the impression that the image has been moved, Speed Pan blurs the left and right sides of the image.
- The Zoom Burst Effect gives the impression that you zoomed in on the subject just before taking the photo.

Special Edits

To create the illusion of selective wide-aperture, shallow-focus effects, you may use Depth of Field to blur a portion of an image.

- One tool that improves the usage of the Recompose tool is Extension Background. Adding backgrounds without leaving any gaps works great.
- You may surround any image with a lovely image with Frame Creator.
- You may utilize the Orton Effect to give a picture an extremely soft-focus appearance. It's pleasant despite having a feel from the 1970s.
- While the Straighten and Crop tools, the Auto Haze Removal tool, and the Spot Healing Brush tidy up the scene, the new Perfect scene function makes it simple to alter any sky. It works effectively and isn't as difficult as it seems. You may also immediately eliminate smoke by selecting Advanced > Enhance.
- Perfect Pet is a feature-rich program that may help you enhance the appearance of photos of your family pets. It allows you to edit photos and has an excellent auto-subject selection capability. This is a fantastic method for improving someone's appearance in a photo. This tool is easy to use and helpful.
- **Recompose:** To alter an image's composition, move and resize user-protected portions of it using the Photomerge engine.
- One tool for choosing and changing text that performs part of the job automatically is called Replace Background. You may utilize one of the backgrounds provided by Elements if you don't have the perfect one. Because it is more difficult for the AI to identify the "right" portions in complicated images, it performs better with simple ones.

- There are several uses for the "Restore Old Photo" feature. In eleven various methods, it may make an antique picture or scanned print seem as if it was shot recently.
- Scratches and Blemishes: Any picture may seem professionally retouched with the aid of the Healing Brush and Spot Healing Brush tools. Many useful utilities.
- You may add creativity to your image by using Text and Border Overlay.
- **Tilt-Shift:** Certain areas of the picture appear unduly soft when the camera is tilted. This gives the impression that the subject is extremely tiny in the image. The majority of video editors come with this well-known function. Shooters may still utilize it now.
- The Water Color Effect is a beautiful layer filter effect that adds a distinctive touch to any image. If you choose to print the artwork on watercolor paper or a comparable medium, it works great.

The photomerge

- You may transfer objects or people between photos with Photomerge Compose. All you have to do is draw a line around the topic. The topic (a person) will then be selected, copied, pasted, and mixed from one image to the next.
- Photomerge Exposure is the Elements effect that most closely resembles a high dynamic range (HDR) effect. It creates an image with more tones than a single snap can manage by combining many frames of the same image. In this situation, HDR tools would do much better.
- When using Photomerge Faces, follow the same steps as when using Photomerge Compose. It is possible to paste a face from one image over another from another. For instance, it works well for group photos when not everyone always grins. It's crucial to keep in mind to purchase more copies of the same group in order to locate suitable "replacements."
- Similar to the Photomerge Faces tool, the Photomerge Group Shot tool is designed for groups of people.
- **Photomerge area Cleaner:** Take many images of a crowded area with the camera still. Then, to remove some of the individuals, copy and paste empty spaces over the congested ones. It works very well and isn't as difficult as it seems.
- Photomerge Panorama's ability to align many images of the same scene to create a seamless panorama is fantastic. If 20% of the image is taken near together, with the same lighting and focal point, it will appear its finest. (Photomerge is only effective if you remember to take many photos.)

The Object Guided Edit for Scaling and Moving

An intriguing, sophisticated, and completely automated picture editing function is not something you discover very frequently. Today, however, is one of those days. The Move & Scale Object option is included in the Guided Edit mode's Basics section.

You could assume that this is simply a huge copy-and-paste effort because of the really great name. It is challenging and may result in editing problems to locate the primary topic, choose it clearly using one of two selection tools, and then copy and paste it to another location in the picture. However, from what I've seen, it only works effectively with rather basic images. Nevertheless, I used this straightforward image of a lady in Egypt photographing the pyramids as an illustration. **Simply follow the on-screen directions to use this function.**

- **Step 1:** The Auto Select tool and the Quick Selection brush are both selection tools from which to pick. Because the second one was simpler to use, I went with it. If there is little contrast in your topic, it may be difficult to get "clean" alternatives. When I made my final decision, I considered a parked automobile in front of the tower and a portion of the blue sky. To copy the text of the selection and then paste it back into the file, I selected the "Duplicate" option. To make it larger, take a corner handle and pull it out. To continue the procedure, click the green checkmark.

- **Step 2:** Next, enlarge the topic. Your pick's precision will be more noticeable as a result. You will have accomplished your goal if you use the Clone Stamp or Spot Healing Brush tool to clear up the digital trickery. The hazy skyline around the pyramids didn't match them, thus I didn't like it.

- **Duplicate option:** When National Geographic editors realize this is their opportunity, they may be frantically looking for coverage. That is an excellent feature for an automated tool since it makes a difficult pick, copy, and paste operation that has a high probability of success very simple.

- **Busy photos:** I made an effort to identify and relocate the lady holding the dog when I snapped this image. As you can see on the right, the selection's outcome was surprisingly decent given how complex the picture was. However, many of the problematic locations seemed to have been erased by the automated healing cover-up process as soon as the item was moved. These kind of errors can be corrected using the Clone Stamp or Healing Brush tools, but it would likely take too long to complete them all in this instance.

The Guided Edit of the Meme Maker

Select an image

Launch Photoshop Elements Editor, and then choose an image to use for your project. You may crop the picture if you like. Next, choose the Guided tab.

Select a Meme Creator

Directly under the Quick/Guided/Advanced menu bars are a few tabs listing all of the guided edit areas. These include the following tabs: Basics, Color, Black & White, Fun Editing, Special Edits, and Photomerge. Elements will open the picture in a box to the right of the image with use instructions once you first choose Fun Edits and then "Meme Maker."

Create the Meme

- Clicking the "Create Meme Template" button will display a frame filled with various colored lights.
- Select "Type Text" from the menu. The text area will seem bold in Photoshop Elements. After you've finished writing, click the green checkmark underneath the text. Click the red Cancel button if you make a mistake.
- The photo that comes with the frame may be resized if you'd like.
- Click on the yellow emblem that resembles the sun. The new window that opens will have additional frames. After selecting the desired frame, click the OK button.
- In addition to shooting a photo, you may add an effect if you'd like.
- When you're ready to continue with the instructions, click the "Next" button at the bottom of the page. In the advanced or rapid edit modes, you have the option to save the meme.

The Panorama Photomerge

Many modern smartphones and tiny cameras include an automated panoramic option since many people like capturing panorama shots. They work most of the time. Because it's so practical, I always use my iPhone for this. Nevertheless, you can never really get the power of a collection of high-resolution images and Elements' Photomerge Panorama for a committed photographer if you simply look at the images taken by your phone, which has a relatively tiny screen. When you save a file and examine it on a large screen, you will see how much more spectacular it may be to have many high-resolution sections joined using Photomerge. It's a very powerful quality. In order to create a panoramic, elements must align and match each region using AI. Each picture must be warped by the program such that the angles, lines, and tones in each section match those in the others. This piece of technology is fantastic when it works properly, which is the majority of the time. Since the process of gathering photos and assembling them into a panorama isn't entirely automated, some preparation needs be done in advance to ensure proper setup.

This is what I believe ought to occur:
- With the camera in program mode, aim the lens at the scene and shoot a test image. Use the Exposure Compensation feature on the camera to adjust the image's brightness if needed.
- If you like the way your left foot appears, take a photo of it and remove the test image.

- Before you begin shooting images, mentally divide the scene into about five vertical sections. Add additional parts if necessary. Start by taking a photo from the frame's left edge. Next, shift the camera to the right until it covers up to 20% of the picture. Lastly, take another photo from that location. Continue doing this until you have covered everything.
- This time, take a picture of your right foot. Even if they were taken months or even years later, this should help you identify those panoramic shots among all the other pictures that were taken at around the same time.
- In Elements, open just those areas.
- After entering the Guided edit section, choose Photomerge>Photomerge Panorama from the menu at the top of the screen.
- To begin, choose every panoramic image using the Photo Bin. Next, choose the "Create panoramic" button located in the lower right corner of the Photomerge application window. After selecting every picture, aligning the edges, and arranging them into a single widescreen image, Elements uses a sophisticated series of black-and-white masks to merge all the components of the images.

Photomerge will ask you whether you want the empty edges to be filled in when the stitching is complete. You will get the pieces since they were captured with a wide-angle lens or perhaps the application itself. The components have been reshaped to improve fit. The cost is reasonable for the breathtaking view. If you choose "Yes," Elements will apply pixels to the empty gaps using its content-aware AI. If you do not wish to do this, you will have to crop the picture to remove any unevenness around the border. In case you need to go back and make any last-minute adjustments, save the image as a Photoshop (.psd) file. Another option would be to save the image as a JPEG after choosing Layer > Flatten Image to reduce the number of layers. The outcome would be the same this way.

After instructing Elements to fill in the borders, I obtained this image. Where Elements has contributed pixels to the design is shown by the dotted selection lines. This is a decent finish, however the yellow tail fin at the rear of the hangar has been duplicated and pasted on top of itself, and there are some odd additional reflections on the floor where none should be. In this example, I cropped the image at the top and bottom and used the Edit>Undo command to remove the AI pixels. The effectiveness of this auto-fill function varies from moment to moment.

Creating a panoramic with many decks

One of the issues you may encounter while piecing everything together is that it might be challenging to print an image that is too broad. This one will be difficult to overcome. It may only be 8 inches high, even if it could be 48 inches wide, particularly if all of your portions were filmed horizontally. You could find a clever and entertaining solution to this issue if you start by zooming in and shooting a lot of cards. This will prevent the picture quality from deteriorating even after cropping.

Cleaner for Photomerge Scenes

Elements first released Photomerge Panorama alone. However, when a few iterations of Elements were released, Photomerge gained further practical applications. The ability to exclude random items and people from a crowded picture was one of these applications to "clean up" the image with a tolerable degree of simplicity. **Do you have a tight deadline?** Scene Cleaner is a function meant to tidy up cluttered and over-filled scenes with the least amount of effort. Copying and pasting is made easy with an automated function. However, for it to function properly, you will need to capture many images of the same topic at the same time.

First, open every picture that was shot there. Choose Photomerge Scene Cleaner from the Guided menu. Scene Cleaner has its own panel, as you may be aware. There is a single picture on the left and a blank area on the right. From the thumbnails at the bottom of the screen with the least amount of clutter, click and drag the picture to the right window. You can click on one of the other thumbnails to change the picture on the left, so don't worry if it's the same as the default one. The picture on the right should be your "working" image. You may begin using everything that Guided Edit has to offer by simply following the excellent instructions that appear on the right side of the screen.

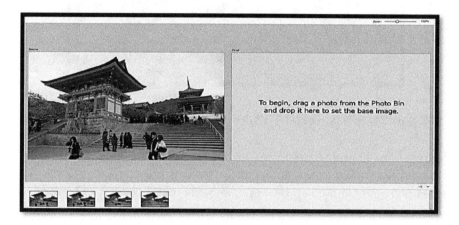

Step 2: I transferred the third picture from the Photo Bin to the window on the right, as seen in this picture. The picture used as the "base" Since the image in both windows is identical; I must alter the image on the left to show the businessman standing at a different location. This will allow me to "clean" them off the right screen. It's crucial to understand that each picture has a hue thanks to its elements. This is a really helpful design decision that will become evident when you have cleaned up the scene by gathering pieces from other images. These four sections are labeled with the following colors: red, green, yellow, and blue.

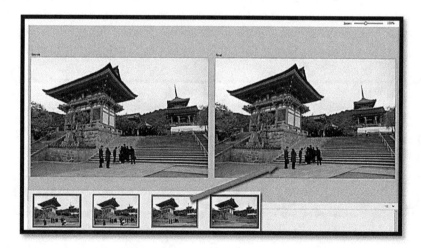

Step 3: There are no people standing in the area where the businesspeople are on the right in the new picture I selected (for the source on the left). You may draw around this area using the Pencil tool, which is located in the menu on the right. The red-coded picture is the source of the

intense red ink employed here. Despite being referred to as a pencil tool, it is really a selection tool.

Step four: this is where the magic begins: The entrepreneurs are hidden when the pixels within the red circle are immediately copied, pasted, and blended over the scene on the right. The fact that you may use Guided without having any prior knowledge of choices, mixing, feathering, or editing in general is one of its finest features. It works flawlessly. Even though the computer does a fantastic job of shifting pixels around, you can see that my red pencil line is not particularly precise.

Step five: cleaning up the remainder of the scene: Since there was nobody on the far left steps, I opted to take the girl mounting the stairs in the picture on the right out of the next frame I selected after doing a fast sketch with the pencil tool. You'll quickly know if you've taken enough shots to make this approach effective. I could have taken a lot more foundation frames on location, but I didn't want to wait twenty minutes for the children to get off the steps. Regardless matter how events unfold, the scene's population has drastically shrunk. To save the file, click the Next button in the lower right corner of the screen. Proceed to the next step in the tag if any modifications are necessary.

Extra Tools: As I said, the pictures were color-coded, and this applies to every picture that was used in the scene-cleaning procedure. The pencil lines you make are reflected in the various hues that highlight images stored in the Photo Bin. To see the portion of the picture that was copied and pasted over the right frame, choose "Show Regions" from the menu on the right side of the screen. When you have a lot of images and the eraser, you may utilize this to assist you make better decisions. On the right side of the screen is the color area. Click the image of the color on the left side of the screen to do this. By doing this, the color will return to the main window's left side.

When the selection "grabs" too many pixels, you should return to the source on the left side of the screen and use the Eraser tool to remove some of the pen markings. This will ensure that it "grabs" fewer pixels when the selection changes. If this doesn't work, I start again with a much smaller pencil tip and erase all the existing pencil lines. Another way to make the selection smaller is to add a little blob to the picture. This will make the selection even smaller. Keep in mind that this is a really simple approach. I doubt you could copy and paste someone's eyes from one photograph to another with this tool, which isn't particularly accurate. The ability to align photographs so that when you copy and paste pixels from one frame over another, they cover the correct region, giving the output the look of being realistic, is another benefit that all Photomerge applications have in common. This is incredibly useful when you're using your hands to take photographs. The Alignment tool won't be necessary if you're using a tripod. Scene Cleaner will align your photographs for you when you launch it. However, you may need to reduce your final picture. This is because during the auto-line-up procedure, some of the originals were shifted from being vertical or horizontal.

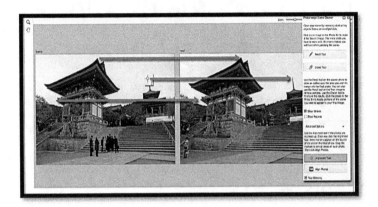

If auto-alignment isn't working properly, use the alignment tool instead. Three line-up target markers must be placed on stationary portions of the picture in the left frame for this to operate. I've enlarged sign #2 in the left window to demonstrate what I mean.) Next, align the targets on the right with the corresponding locations on the left, click Align Photos and Elements will work its magic—which often does a great job. For the Scene Cleaner to function, you must keep in mind to capture the raw material—many frames of the same scene over time—while you are on location. The objective of photographing people is to have them remain still and silent for a brief period of time while three to five images of the same subject are taken, ensuring that individuals move between photos.

The Action Panel

The Actions panel in Photoshop Elements provides a multitude of choices and makes it easy to record, play, modify, and remove specific actions. To see the Actions Panel, you must be in Advanced mode. Click the Advanced button at the top of the page to do this. By selecting Window > Actions, you may access the Actions panel in Photoshop Elements, which contains the list of actions. You can load.atn files created in Adobe Photoshop, but you cannot create your own action files in Photoshop Elements. Once an image is created, it may be altered in several ways using these files. To make them easier to manage, groups of related activities are arranged in a deliberate manner. An action file must first be opened before it can be used on an image. If the Actions box isn't visible currently, choose Actions from the Window menu. Users may choose an action by clicking on it in the Actions panel, or they can open an Action Set by clicking on the triangle icon. To launch the program, you may either choose the Play option from the Actions panel menu or push the Play button on the panel. Generally speaking, the Actions panel in Photoshop Elements' Advanced mode is a strong tool that enables users to swiftly edit and enhance images by executing pre-configured actions or actions that import them from Adobe Photoshop.

95

CHAPTER NINE
ABOUT TYPOGRAPHY AND TEXT
Knowing the Fundamentals of Type

Elements include seven Type tools. Two of them are for inputting horizontally laid-out type, while the other two are for vertically laid-out type. Don't worry about the vertical tools. You can use them, but they can write Chinese and Japanese characters since they were designed with Asian users in mind. You may type on a selection, shape, or path with the final three tools. A route is a line—straight or curved—that your text follows but that is not visible in the picture.

About Type tools

I will just discuss the two horizontal type tools here since the vertical and horizontal type tools are identical. **I refer to them as the Type and Type Mask tools to make things simple:**
- **Type:** Enter type using this tool. Unless it is used in bitmap mode or index color mode, which do not support layers, this type is created on its type layer.
- **Type Mask:** This tool creates a selection boundary in the form of the type you want to input rather than actual type. The selection edge has now been added to the active layer. You can accomplish whatever you can with any other selection while using a type selection.

Three further type tools exist, each of which creates type on a route in a unique manner:
- **Text on Selection:** This tool allows you to draw on a picture to select it, much as the Quick Selection tool. It transforms the choice into a route. When you add words, it takes on the form of the road.
- **Text on form:** You may draw any form from the shapes menu with this tool. When you add a shape, the text travels with it.
- **Text on Custom route:** You may create whatever route you choose on your picture with the Text on Custom Path tool. Text entered on the special route remains on that path.

All three path-type tools create a type layer

Anchor points, straight segments, and curved segments are the three components that make up a route. The trail hovers above the picture in its own "space," without altering or leaving any traces. The route in this instance is only a cable that the text may follow. You may modify the route to your preference using the Refine route option.

The Modes

You may insert text in Elements in three different ways: point, paragraph, and path. Both the Type and Type Mask tools allow you to alternate between point and paragraph mode.

See the sections that follow for a detailed breakdown of each style and the steps involved in composing the text:

- **Point:** Only a few words should be entered in this setting. After clicking on your picture, use the Type tool and start typing. The content appears as you enter and continues to grow in length. Furthermore, it extends beyond the boundaries of your picture! A new line does not get point type. To get to the next line, you must hit Enter (or Return on a Mac).
- **Paragraph:** You may add lengthier text passages to a picture using this method. To create a box around the text, click and drag the type tool, then type. It is a resizable box that contains all of the writing. Elements will transfer a line of text to the next line for you if it is too lengthy.
- **Route:** Text may be positioned along a route using three distinct type tools in Elements. The text appears following the path's form when you double-click on it and start typing.

Formats

Elements can display and print text in two distinct forms. Your requirements will determine the format you select. **Every format has benefits and drawbacks. What you should know about them both:**

- **Vector:** All of the text in Elements is first created as a vector type. In vector type, you may alter the outline size without causing the borders of the vertical strokes to seem jagged. Vector type is still completely editable and prints at the best quality, appearing neat and clear. Elements will utilize the vector type format for images that are not in Bitmap or Index Color mode.
- **Raster:** Text is rasterized in Elements when vector type is converted to pixels. This rasterization procedure is referred to as "simplifying" by Elements. Text is simplified by being converted to a raster picture, which prevents text editing. You generally make things easier when you want to integrate the type with an image or apply filters to your vector type to make it seem a specific manner. Simplified type cannot be resized without sacrificing part of its elegance or giving the corners a harsh appearance.

Establishing Point Type

Point type is most likely the mode in which you type the most. Taglines, logos, headlines, and the headers of web pages are examples of brief language that works well with point type. The fact that point type only has one anchor point, which signifies the start of the line of type, gives it its name. Remember that lines of the point type do not wrap by default.

Point type doesn't wra

Do the following to create a point type:
- When you launch the Photo Editor, choose the "Advanced" setting.
- To create a new, empty Elements file or open an image, choose File > New > Blank File and click OK.
- The Tools panel has the Horizontal Type tool. Choose it.
- To move between the various type tools, you may also hit the T key. You may also choose the Horizontal Type tool from the Tool Options. The letter T seems to be what it is.
- To put the text into the picture, click on it. Your cursor is known as an I-beam. You create an insertion point when you click. A tiny, horizontal line that extends around one-third of the way up the I-beam serves as the baseline for horizontal type. The content continues here.
- To choose your type choices, use the Tool options.
- Type your text and hit Enter (or Return on a Mac) to begin a new line. When you hit Enter (or Return), the hard return you entered remains in place.
- Click the "Commit" button, which resembles a blue checkmark, next to your text to save it. To exit, click the Cancel button (the blue X). To commit the type, you may alternatively hit Enter on the numeric keypad or choose any other tool in the Tools menu. With your writing on it, a new kind of layer is created. You can see that you have type layers in the Layers panel by looking at the T symbol on your screen.

Constructing a Paragraph Type

If you have lengthier text sections, it is usually more convenient to compose them in paragraph format. Although the content is confined inside a box, entering paragraph type is similar to entering text in a word processor or page layout tool. When you type to the end of the box, the text is automatically wrapped to the next line.

To enter the paragraph type, follow these steps:
- When you launch the Photo Editor, choose the "Advanced" setting.
- To create a new, empty Elements file or open an image, choose File > New > Blank File and click OK.
- To switch between the various type tools, press T or choose the Horizontal Type tool from the Tools menu.
- You may also choose the Horizontal Type tool from the Tool Options.
- **There are two methods to add and modify the image's bounding box size:**
  - To create a bounding box that is almost the size you want, drag. You may adjust the size of the box by dragging any of its sides or corners when you release the mouse button.
  - Holding down the Alt key (or Option on a Mac), click the picture. The Paragraph Text Size option box appears. Enter the precise dimensions of the box you want to enclose. The box you selected appears with handles that you may use to adjust its size later when you click OK.

- To choose your type choices, use the Tool options. Enter your text here. Press Enter (or Return on a Mac) to start a new paragraph. To fit within the bounding box, each line completely encircles it. If you input more text than the text box can accommodate, an overflow symbol will appear, which a box with a plus sign is within. You may adjust the text box's size by dragging a border box handle.
- The "Commit" button is shown by the blue checkmark symbol next to the text field. Hit it. "Enter" is another keyboard shortcut.
- The "Cancel" button, which resembles a blue X, allows you to restart. A new type layer is created by elements whenever you press "Commit."

Paragraph type wraps automatically without your assistance, so there's no need to enter a hard return as you type.

Establishing a Path Type

If you want your type to flow in any shape—a circle, a wave, a stair step, or something else entirely—you're in luck. You can accomplish it using the three type tools that Elements provides. The route type not only resides on its layer, which is fantastic, but it is also simple to create, modify, and move about.

Using the tool for Text on Selection

You must first choose your picture before you can create a route type. This is comparable to the Quick Selection tool's selection process. How to accomplish it:
- When you launch the Photo Editor, choose the "Advanced" setting.
- To create a new, empty Elements file or open an image, choose File > New > Blank File and click OK.
- Select the Text on Selection tool from the Tools menu. To move between the various type tools, you may also hit the T key. You may also use the Text on Selection tool from the Tool Options. It appears like a capital T surrounded by a square of dots.
- Drag your finger over the selection you want to "paint" on the picture.
- Use one of four methods to refine your selection by adding or deleting from it:

- ➢ To add the extra region to your selection, use the Shift key and drag it around.
- ➢ To remove an area from your selection on a Mac, hit the Alt key and drag it around.
- ➢ Drag around the regions you want to include after selecting the "Add to Selection" or "Subtract from Selection" buttons in the Tool Options.
- ➢ To make your pick larger or smaller, drag the Offset slider in the Tool Options to the right or left. Additional settings that are shared by all type tools may be specified.
- ♣ Click the "Commit" button, which resembles a blue check mark, to make your pick a route. Click the blue "X" (Cancel) to restart.
- ♣ Over the route, place the pointer. Click on the path and input your content when the cursor icon transforms to an I-beam, which resembles a capital I with a crooked line across it. The road is completely encircled by the words. If you write more text than the route can contain, an overflow indicator appears. Adjust the selection's size so all of your text is visible.
- ♣ Click the "Commit" button, which resembles a blue checkmark, to save your work. Elements create a new type layer. Any property, including font and size, may be changed, just like point or paragraph text.

Using the tool for Text on Shape

The Text On form tool allows you to create text that wraps around the borders of any form. The actions you must do are as follows:
- ♣ When you launch the Photo Editor, choose the "Advanced" setting.
- ♣ To create a new, empty Elements file or open an image, choose File > New > Blank File and click OK.
- ♣ To move between the various type tools, press T or choose the Text On Shape tool from the Tools menu.
- ♣ You may also use the Text on Shape tool from the Tool Options. It resembles a T with a wavy box around it.
- ♣ In the Tool Options, choose the desired form from the list of shapes.
- ♣ **Drag your tool over the picture to make the shape.**
  - ➢ To limit your dimensions, hold down the Shift key while dragging.
  - ➢ To draw from the center outward, hold down the Alt (or Option on a Mac) key while dragging.
- ♣ Over the route, place the pointer. Click on the path and input your content when the cursor icon transforms to an I-beam, which resembles a capital I with a crooked line across it. The text encircles the shape's trajectory. If you write more text than the route can contain, an overflow indicator appears. Modify the route till your whole text appears.
- ♣ Click the "Commit" button, which resembles a blue checkmark, to save your work. To restart, click the blue "X" (Cancel) symbol. Elements create a new type layer. Any property, including font and size, may be changed, just like point or paragraph text. Additionally, you may alter the shape by selecting the desired alteration under Image > Transform Shape.

You may further personalize your form path by using the Modify tool, which appears in the Tool Options when you choose the Text On Custom Path tool. Make sure your type layer is selected in the Layers panel before utilizing this option.

Using the tool for Text on Custom Path

You may create your own path or shape to serve as the foundation for your type using the Text on Custom Path tool. How to accomplish it:

- When you launch the Photo Editor, choose the "Advanced" setting.
- To create a new, empty Elements file or open an image, choose File > New > Blank File and click OK.
- Select the Text on Custom Path tool from the Tools menu. To move between the various type tools, you may also hit the T key. You may also use the Text On Custom Path tool from the Tool Options. It seems to have a line through a T.
- By moving your tool over the picture, you may create whatever route you like. Click the "Commit" button to complete the journey.
- Choose the Modify tool (the arrow icon) from the Tool Options to fine-tune your route. Use the tool to drag the anchor points or path components to create the desired form.
- Over the route, place the pointer. Click on the path and input your content when the cursor icon transforms to an I-beam, which resembles a capital I with a crooked line across it. The text follows the shape's trajectory. If you write more text than the route can contain, an overflow indicator appears. Modify the route as needed to ensure that all of the content appears. Remember that after you've input your kind, you may still alter the course. After choosing Image>Transform Shape, choose a command from the list of alternatives, such Free Transform Shape.
- Click the blue checkmark symbol that reads "Commit." Click the blue "Cancel" icon to start again after typing your content. Elements create a new type layer. Any property, including font and size, may be changed, just like point or paragraph text.
- To create a new custom route, choose the background layer in the Layers panel and repeat Steps 3–7.

Choosing Type Options

The Type tool is found in the Tool Options box, which is at the bottom of the workspace, as shown in the figure below. There are many character and paragraph-type options in this box. Using these options, you may choose the sort of picture you want to use and match it with your photographs.

Each option in the Tool Options is described as follows:
- **Font Family:** Select the desired font from the drop-down menu. Elements has a font menu that is WYSIWYG (What You See Is What You Get). The term Sample is shown in the real font after each font name, so you no longer have to choose a font without seeing how it appears. **Before each font name, one of these acronyms additionally indicates the kind of font:**
  - ➢ A: Adobe Type 1 typefaces (PostScript)
  - ➢ TT: typefaces of TrueType
  - ➢ O: OpenType typefaces

Because bitmapped typefaces lack abbreviations, each word is composed of several dots, thus scaling may be challenging. Use OpenType, TrueType, or PostScript fonts wherever feasible. Note that you can also notice a Tk abbreviation if you use Adobe Creative Cloud. This refers to Typekit (formerly Adobe Fonts), a free typeface collection available online.
- **Font Style:** Certain font families include additional styles, such as condensed and light. Only the styles that work with a certain typeface are shown in the list. Additionally, this menu is WYSIWYG.
- **Font Size:** Type a font size in the box or choose your favorite using the drop-down menu. Type size is most often measured in points. One inch is equivalent to 72 points at a level of 72 ppi. You may switch the units to pixels or centimeters by selecting Edit > Preferences > Units & Rulers (or, if you're using a Mac, choose Adobe Photoshop Elements Editor > Preferences > Units & Rulers).
- **Leading:** The term "leading" refers to the space between the baselines of type lines; it is pronounced "LED-ding." A baseline is the imaginary line on which a line of type rests. Either choose "Auto Leading" or specify how much leading it should perform on its own. Elements utilizes a value that is 120% of the size of your type point when you choose Auto Leading. The 10-point kind so has a 12-point advantage. In order to prevent the very tops of the extremely tall letters on the next line from colliding with the bottoms of the very low characters, elements add that additional 20%.

- **Tracking:** The distance between letters in a group is altered by this new setting. The letters are closer together when the quantity is negative and further away when it is positive.
- **Color:** Click the color swatch in the Color Picker to choose a color for your type. Additionally, you may choose a color in the Swatches tab.
- **Faux Bold:** You may create a bold style with this option if there isn't one already (you'd choose it under Font Style). Remember that applying false styles may alter font sizes, but don't worry, it won't happen. Real-style typefaces are what you should use. It's okay if there are none.
- **Faux Italic:** This option has the same warning as Faux Bold and creates a fake oblique style.
- **Underline:** Your type is clearly highlighted by this setting, such as this.
- **Strikethrough:** Select this option if you want your text to seem to have lines running through it.
- **Text Alignment:** There are three options for aligning horizontal text: left, right, or center. These choices will rotate 90 degrees clockwise and switch to top, bottom, and center vertical settings if you have text that is moving up or down.
- **Style:** By choosing this option, a drop-down panel with pre-made layer styles for your Type will appear. Once you have committed your kind, you may utilize this option.
- **Modify Text Orientation:** Click this option after selecting the type layer to modify the text orientation. This will allow you to choose between type orientations that are vertical and horizontal.
- **Warped Text:** This entertaining feature allows you to alter the type's form in over a dozen distinct ways.
- **Anti-aliasing:** Your text will have somewhat smoother edges if you choose this option. Should you choose "Anti-aliasing," that edge will be one pixel softer. This setting should be left on the majority of the time. In situations when you wish to display tiny text on the screen, such as on web sites, you may want to disable it. Because the borders are so soft, it might sometimes be difficult to read.
- **Text Overlay Templates:** The Quote Graphic dialog box will popup when you choose this option. You may include text, images, and effects in this area.

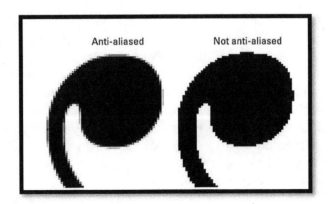

103

Type settings may be applied either before or after typing. You may utilize the new Guided Edit called Add Text to quickly and easily add stylish text to your photographs if all of these options seem like too much effort.

Text Editing

To correct errors, add or delete type, or modify any of the type settings, just follow these steps:

- Select the Type tool from the Tools menu.
- Double-clicking within the text will automatically choose the type layer. Note that selecting all of the text requires three clicks.
- **Modify your wording in any way:**
  - ➢ Modify the font's size, color, family, and other characteristics. If you want to alter all of the text, choose that type layer in the Layers window. To highlight certain portions of the text, select it and move the Type tool's I-beam across it. Choose your changes in the Tool Options.
  - ➢ **Remove the text.** To highlight the text, drag the Type tool's I-beam over it. Next, hit your Mac's Delete (Backspace) key.
  - ➢ **Include text.** To create an entrance point, click your I-beam within the text line. Type your new text after that.

Note: Any text type, including point, paragraph, and path text, may be edited using these procedures.

- When you're done modifying your text, click the "Commit" blue check mark symbol. Sometimes you may also need to change your text. To accomplish this, choose the type layer in the Layers menu. Next, choose Transform > Image > Free Transform. Grasp the edges of the box and move them to rotate or scale. Press Ctrl (or cmd on a Mac) and drag a handle to adjust the form. Double-clicking within the box or clicking the Commit button—which resembles a blue checkmark button—will preserve the changes.

Type Simplifying

Elements can display and print two different forms: raster and vector. As long as the type is on a type layer and stored as a vector file, you may alter and modify it at any time. However, there are situations when you may need to simplify your type, which entails converting it into dots. After simplifying it, you may use colors and patterns, paint the text, and apply filters. Combining all of a picture's layers into a single backdrop image is known as flattening. This indicates that your font layer has been simplified and blended in with the image's other pixels. Additionally, Elements will inform you that the type layer has to be simplified before you can apply a filter to it. To simplify the layer, click OK; to halt the operation, click Cancel. Choose the type layer in the Layers panel, then pick Layer>Simplify Layer. Your type will be simpler to read as a result. After that, your type layer is transformed (the T symbol vanishes) into a standard layer, displaying your type as pixels on a clear backdrop.

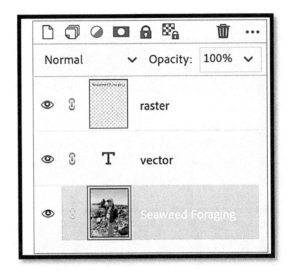

Before simplifying, make any necessary changes to avoid having to start your type from scratch. This includes the size of your words. You can't adjust the text's size without obtaining the dreaded jaggies after you simplify your font. Another drawback of simplified type is that, although seeming the same online, it never prints as sharply and cleanly as vector type. Even at larger sizes, the edges of simplified type are usually a little ragged. For this reason, if you want to attempt painting or applying filters to your text layer, you need first create a duplicate of it before simplifying it and then hide it.

Using Type Mask

The ideal method for combining type and picture is to use the Type Mask tool. Unlike the Type tool, the Type Mask tool does not create a new layer. As an alternative, it selects the currently chosen layer. Type Mask is the finest tool to use if you want to fill text with a picture or remove text from an image so that the backdrop is visible. A selection is a selection regardless of how it was made. Despite seeming like letters, type mask options act as selections. They are movable, editable, and saveable. **To make a type mask, follow these steps:**

+ Open the desired picture in the Advanced mode of the Photo Editor.
+ To turn your backdrop into a layer, double-click the term backdrop in the Layers menu and choose OK. Following this, you may style the type to improve its appearance.
+ Select the Horizontal Type Mask tool from the Tools menu.
+ Choose your type settings (such as Font Family, Style, and Size) under the Tool Options.
+ Click the picture, and then type the text of your choice. When you're finished, click the "Commit" button with the blue check mark. A selection border in the form of your type appears in your picture.
+ Selecting choose>Inverse will choose every other option and deselect your letter selections.
+ Use Backspace (or Delete on a Mac) to remove anything that is not in your selection. Your picture has now filled your type.

- Select, then Deselect.
- **Try applying several layer styles to your typography.**
  - ➢ You may choose Window > Styles or click the Styles button at the bottom of the screen.
  - ➢ Choose the desired layer style, such as Drop Shadows or Bevels, from the drop-down option at the top of the panel.
  - ➢ Click on the desired style to choose it.

The picture below has a simple inner bevel and a drop shadow. Create a new layer, choose Edit > Fill Layer, and then use the Use drop-down option to select the color you want, just as I did. Your type will be seen against a solid backdrop as a result.

Making masked text is made considerably simpler by the Photo Text Guided Edit, which is seen in the figure below. Click on the Fun Edits tab when in Guided Edit mode, then follow the simple instructions. This change also makes it simple to add a shadow, curve, or stroke. Located under Fun Edits, this is the Multi-Photo Text Guided Edit. You may use a separate picture for each word of your sentence if you feel that one image is insufficient!

Warping and Stylizing Type

If you have ever created a type mask, you are aware that Elements is capable of much more than just adding a few black letters on an image's bottom. Additionally, with a few clicks here and there, you may enhance style, distort, and stretch your type. If you're not cautious, creative typography might detract from the importance of your picture.

Modifying the type's opacity

Choose the type layer whose opacity you want to alter in the Layers panel. Next, move the slider by clicking the arrow to the right of the opacity percentage. It is also possible to provide a number in the Opacity box. When the percentage is low, more of the layer underneath is visible since the type is less thick.

Using filters for your category

Using filters and other intriguing effects is one of the nicest things you can do with type-in elements that you can't accomplish with a word processor or page layout tool. As you can see in the pictures below, you may apply a motion blur to give the impression that the text is moving, burning, or submerged. The sole need is that the type be abbreviated before a filter may be applied. Wait until you have completed modifying the text before proceeding to the filtering step. Simply choose the Layers panel's simplified type layer from the Filter menu, then click on it to apply the filter.

Using color and gradients to paint your typography

Text may be easily changed by selecting it and using the Color Picker to choose a color. But what if you'd want to attempt something a little different, like using arbitrary brushstrokes to paint the type? The sole need this time is that the type must be simplified, much as when you apply filters to text. Choose a color, pick up the Brush tool, adjust the parameters, and then paint. For our example, I selected the Granite Flow brush from the Special Effect Brushes settings. I just swiped our type a few times while using a diameter of 39, 15, and 6 pixels.

You may also give your font a gradient. Once your type has been simplified, do these actions:
- You may either lock the transparency of the layer in the Layers panel or Ctrl-click (or cmd-click on a Mac) the layer containing the text to select it.
- The Tools panel has the Gradient tool. Choose it.
- Click the down arrow next to the Gradient Picker in the Tool Options to bring up the Gradient Picker panel.
- Select the desired gradient.
- Drag your gradient pointer to the desired end of the gradient after positioning it where you want the gradient to start on the text.

Dissatisfied with the result? Continue dragging until you get the desired effect. You can drag over categories, in any direction, and for any period of time.

Warping your type

Try using the Warp tool if you dislike the way text is shown in a straight line. The nicest part about the modifications you make is that, after they are applied, you may still make adjustments to the text. This component is easy to use and enjoyable. Click the "Create Warped Text" option in the Tool Options. (This opens the Warp Text dialog box.) It's the T with the curved line underneath it. There are several distortions with names like Bulge, Inflate, and Squeeze on the Style drop-down list. Once you've chosen a warp style, you may drag the sliders to adjust the orientation, bend, and distortion level. The amount of warp is altered by the Bend setting, while the warp's appearance from various perspectives is altered by the Horizontal and Vertical Distortions. It's useful that you can see the outcomes as you make adjustments. I could go into more detail about these adjustments, but you have to test them out for yourself to see what they do.

Using Templates for Text Overlays

Click this button, and then follow the steps below to add text and images to your picture.

- Click the Text Overlay Templates button in the Tool Options when the Type tool is chosen.
- **In the Quote Graphic dialog box, you have the following options:**
  - ➢ **Start from Scratch:** This option allows you to choose a standard picture size, such as that of a letter or Instagram post, among other things. Upon selecting OK, a blank design will appear. In the Backgrounds section on the right, you may choose an existing backdrop or choose one from your computer or Organizer. A border may be added; choose the color and size. You may flip the picture as well. You may alter the default text to the word of your choice by clicking the text box. You may alter the text's font, size, alignment, and other characteristics under the Styles panel. You may add shapes and graphics to your picture with the aid of their many panels. Simply click on the desired shape or picture to add it. When you're finished, click Save to name and save your work. Clicking "Done" will return you to the Editor.
  - ➢ **"Start with a Photo":** If you have a picture open and would want to add text to it, click here. Next, follow the identical steps you took when you first began.
  - ➢ **Select one of the many pre-made templates:** After selecting a template, select the desired picture size. Then proceed as you would if you were working with a photo or beginning from scratch. A completed picture may be seen below.

CHAPTER TEN

MOBILE COMPANION APPS AND WEBSITES (BETA)

Using companion mobile applications (beta) and the web

By enabling you to access, view, create, and share your images and videos from any location, the companion applications for the web and mobile devices that come with Adobe Photoshop Elements 2025 are designed to make editing them simpler. **Make use of them as follows:**

Beta Web Companion App

- ♣ Access Anywhere: Use any browser to launch the online application to see your projects.
- ♣ Create and Edit: Use basic editing tools to make rapid adjustments to your images and movies.
- ♣ Share and Collaborate: Sharing your work and collaborating on projects with others is simple.

Beta Mobile Companion App

- ♣ **Upload to Cloud:** The mobile app allows you to upload images and videos to the cloud. The desktop and browser applications may then be used to see them.
- ♣ **Fast Edits:** Auto-crop and auto-fix are examples of one-click rapid operations.
- ♣ **View and Share:** You may use your mobile device to access, view, and share your images and videos.

Paid users of Photoshop Elements 2025 can download these companion apps, which are currently in beta testing.

Instructions for Installation

We're launching a mobile application that utilizes Premiere and Photoshop elements. Using the PC apps to perform more complex edits after sharing images and videos to the cloud is made simple by this app. The public beta version of the app is accessible to authorized users of:

- Desktop programs Photoshop Elements 2025 and Premiere Elements 2025
- Desktop programs Photoshop Elements 2024 and Premiere Elements 2024
- The desktop programs Photoshop Elements 2023 and Premiere Elements 2023

You can also try the mobile apps for free for seven days. Android v9 or later and iOS 14.5 or later are compatible with the app. **With the Adobe Elements beta app on your phone, you can do the following:**

- Store images and videos in the cloud for viewing on the PC and Elements web apps.
- Obtain images and videos, view them, and distribute.
- Auto Crop, Auto Straighten, Auto Tone, Auto White Balance, and Remove Background are one-click Quick Actions for photos.
- You can use simple editing tools to crop, rotate, transform, and alter the aspect ratio of images.
- Making adjustments to images, including temperature, tint, vibrance, saturation, highlights, shadows, exposure, contrast, and more.
- Create Auto Background, Pattern Overlay, and Moving Overlay artwork with your own images.
- In Photoshop Elements 2025, you may import images and movies from your phone's gallery by scanning a QR code.
- You can store up to 2GB of photos and movies in the cloud for free.

How to set up the beta Android app

A. Either scan the QR code below or hit the Google Play store icon to open the app on your Android phone. You can look for the app on Google Play as well.

B. Enter your Adobe ID to get into the application. You don't need a redemption code or serial number.

C. **Once you've tried the app, do let us know your thoughts. You can give comments in any of the following ways:**

> o   Adobe forums
> o   The feedback area within the app.
> o   Email
> o   Private ratings and feedback via Google Play.

How to install the iOS beta app

For the iOS companion app to install, you'll need Apple TestFlight. Apple only permits 10,000 users at a time to access the Adobe Elements mobile companion app, which is currently under beta testing. If the number of downloads has been met, you'll be told that you can't access the app.

Here's how to get started:

⬇ To access to TestFlight from your iOS phone, tap on the Apple App Store icon or scan the QR code below. Then, follow the on-screen steps to download and install the app.

⬇ Using the UI of the TestFlight app, install the Adobe Elements iOS app.

⬇ Open the Adobe Elements iOS app and use your Adobe ID to sign in. You will be alerted by TestFlight whenever a new build of your app is available, and it will also tell you what's new in that release. Installing the newest builds is easy if you have TestFlight 3 or later. Just switch on automatic updates. Please let us know what you think about the app once you've tried it.

You may offer comments in any of the following ways:

> o Adobe forums
>
> o The feedback area within the app
>
> o Email

Editing photos on the go using mobile app features

The Photoshop Elements mobile app lets you edit while you're on the go. It will affect the way you are creative. You may utilize its power in this way:

- **Rapid Edits:** With only a touch, you can perform rapid modifications like auto-crop, brightness, and color tweaks.
- **Filters and Effects:** Choose from several filters and effects to instantly make your images seem better.
- **Crop and Rotate:** You can effortlessly crop and move your photographs to achieve the finest arrangement.
- **Text and Overlays:** You may add text and interesting overlays to your images directly from your phone.
- **Upload and Sync:** When you upload photographs to the cloud, ensure sure they are synchronized across all of your devices so you can update them without any hassles.

CHAPTER ELEVEN

IMPROVEMENTS AND ARTISTIC EFFECTS

The Filter Menu

There are several filter effects available in the Filter menu. Some of them are designed to give your work a sophisticated appearance. To alter the form, draw, style, add color, and even create additional digital noise, I use effects. I utilize some to blur pixels (for depth of field effects). Any filter effect may be placed within a pick and applied to either the whole image or just a portion of it. **Examine these filter choices:**

+ **Correct Camera Distortion**: only lens distortion can be corrected with this filter, which makes it special. This allows you to create a scenario, alter the point of view, and add or eliminate visual defects.

+ **Filter gallery:** This option allows you to see the appearance of all the filter effects before using them. Only 8-bit pictures may be used with this option. To locate this option, choose "filter gallery" from the "File" menu. Clicking on this option in the filter gallery will bring up a conversation window. The "filter category" folder may then be selected. In the "filter category," if you click on the folder you desire, the other effects inside it will be shown. You may choose from a variety of alternatives under the "Artistic" filter box, including colored, dry brush, film grain, drawing, and more. When you click on the drop-down menu, alternatives are shown. If you click on it again, it will shut.

By adjusting the options on the right side of the sample panel, you may customize the filter's appearance. When you're finished, click "OK" to exit the chat window. Click the "new effect layer button" at the bottom of the screen to apply several filters to your image or artwork. Clicking this button copies the filter you just used. Select the filter effect you want to remove from the list at the bottom of the chat window. After that, use the "delete effect layer button."

The Blur Filter

It blurs a picture's pixels in the same manner as the blur tool. The most popular tool under this choice is Gaussian Blur, but you may also choose other blur kinds, such lens blur, motion blur, and more, from the tool's flyout menu. This is most effective when masks are used. People employ a wide variety of different possibilities. One of these effects is "iris blur," which creates a little depth of focus. Simply place the pin where you want to concentrate to utilize it.

Warp

This option allows you to apply some nice effects. Clicking on most of the "distort filter" choices opens a chat window with more options. The following are the choices on the flyout menu:

- **Displace:** The "Displace" option allows us to alter a selection's form. You may, for example, make an image seem to have been distorted and written on a surface held by its corners.
- **Pinch:** Using this filter will result in a selection. The negative number travels away from the center, whereas the positive number advances in its direction.
- The image is converted from rectangular to polar coordinates and back again using this filter. You may adjust the amount of blurring by adjusting the parameters.
- **Ripple:** This filter transforms an image or a portion of an image to resemble waves. The quantity and size of waves may be altered using a variety of settings.
- **Shear:** This filter modifies the appearance of an image as it follows a curve. By moving the line on the box above, you may alter the curve's form. To return to the straight line, click "default". For sections that are fuzzy, there are two options: "wrap-around" and "repeat edge pixels."
- **Spherize:** This filter gives the image a three-dimensional appearance by wrapping it around a sphere.
- **Twirl:** The pick is turned more sharply in the center by this filter than it is on the edges. The direction of the twirl is up to you.
- **Wave:** Although this effect resembles spin, there are many more methods to modify it. You may alter a variety of parameters to fine-tune your filter, including frequency, wave height, wave type, and the number of wave creators.
- **Zig Zag:** This filter gives the selection or picture a crooked appearance.

About Noise

This filter has the ability to add or remove noise. The noise fly-out box has a few filters.

- **Include Noise:** This will add a few arbitrary pixels to the image. The "amount" tool may be moved to alter the number of pixels. The two sharing choices that are available are Gaussian and regular.

> The uniform distribution seems more even, while the Gaussian distribution appears splotchier. There is a "monochromatic" button underneath these choices. Although it is seldom checked, if you do, your photo's pixels will be colored.

- **Despeckle:** This filter searches for edges or areas where there has been a significant color shift. Other than those boundaries, everything is hazy. This fixes the image while preserving the details.
- **Dust and Scratch filter:** This reduces eye strain by altering pixels that seem too similar. Its operation may be altered by adjusting the trigger and radius parameters.
- **Median filter:** This filter discovers pixels that are about the same brightness and eliminates pixels that vary too much from the pixels behind and next to them. The average brightness of a few pixels is then substituted for the middle pixels. As a result, the image seems to have been sketched. By dragging the circle tool around, you may alter its appearance.
- **Reduce Noise:** This improves the overall appearance of the image by lowering the brightness and color noise.

Pixelate

This filter skews the image by placing dots with the same color value in the same cells. For this filter, the flyout window offers a few possibilities. These filters are called Mezzotint, Facet, Crystallize, Pointillize, and Color Halftone. But "Mosaic Filter" is the most popular and effective method of pixelating. The images are grouped into blocks when you apply this filter. When you click on this one, a box containing choices with a "cell size" slider will appear. As we increase the size of the cells, the square boxes increase in size. Tiny boxes of the same hue indicate the filter that is being used.

Filter for Rendering

You may create clouds, strands, lens flares, and lighting effects, among other things, using this filter.

Filters to be sharpened

This filter may be used to highlight hazy images and increase the visibility of the pixels next to them. The flyout menu of this filter has a lot of possibilities.

- The option "Sharpen and sharpen more" allows you to immediately sharpen the image, improving it. Your image will appear much better with the "Sharpen more" option than it would with only the "Sharpen" option.
- **Sharpen Edges:** This filter allows you to sharpen an image's edges while maintaining the image's overall level of smoothness or blur.
- **Unsharpen Mask:** To make the image seem sharper, this effect inserts a line of brighter and darker colors on each side of the edges and alters their contrast.

- **Smart Sharpen:** Selecting this option will open a chat window with several buttons and options. You may adjust how clear an image has to be using the "amount" slider in this option.
- The size of the picture will be determined by the following slider. It's called "radius." If the radius is too tiny, the little particle will stick out more in the noise. Larger objects will be more noticeable if the radius is larger.

Cut down on noise. Adding sharpness may generate a lot of noise, as you may discover. The noise level is decreased by selecting the "reduce noise" option. Increasing the "reduce noise" setting will also eliminate the sharpness.

Style

This is due to the fact that this filter shifts the pixels and intensifies the highlights. It gives the image a captivating appearance. The flyout menu for this filter has a few choices.

- **Diffuse:** This filter makes the focus less obvious by shifting the pixels in the image. This option allows you to choose from four different modes.
  - ➢ **Normal:** ignores the color values and moves the pixels at random.
  - ➢ **Dark Only:** Use the darker pixels to swap out the lighter ones.
  - ➢ **Only Lighten:** Swap out the darker pixels with lighter ones.
  - ➢ **Anisotropic:** This setting swaps out the pixels in the direction where color changes the least.
- **Emboss:** This filter will give the image a stamped appearance. The stamping angle, height, percentage, and quantity are among the choices available in the conversation box of this filter. It gives the impression that the picture has been "extruded from the surface" by turning its fill color gray and tracing the edges with the original fill color.
- **Extrude:** This filter gives the image a three-dimensional appearance. There are two ways to extrude the image: blocks and pyramids. The size and depth of the blocks and stacks are evident.
- **Find Edges:** To highlight the picture's edges on a lighter backdrop, this filter added black lines around them. As a result, the image seemed to be a drawing.
- **Solarize:** This filter creates a photo by combining the positive and negative (and so upside-down) images.
- **Tiles:** The images are separated into many tiles by this filter. With this filter, you can choose the maximum distance and the quantity of tiles.
- Trace Contour: The main shift in brightness of the picture is followed by tiny lines of a distinct color for each color channel. The Trace Contour filter does this.
- **Wind:** To create the illusion that the wind swept the image away, this filter applies thin lines across the image.

Additional Filters

- **Custom:** This option allows you to create your own filter.
- **High Pass:** This filter enhances the visibility of edges by making them more noticeable. You may adjust the sharpness of the edges of its speech bubble with the radius tool.

Since this filter converts the fill color to a single gray hue, it is best used in the "overlay" mix mode.

- **Maximum and Minimum:** These effects allow you to create the illusion that the picture is being stretched or compressed. The black and white components are compressed when the strongest filter is used. Using the tiniest filter results in black and white specks that are compressed together.
- Offset Filter: By repeatedly recording your image, you may create patterns that never stop. With this filter, your images will be shifted to the left or right by a certain amount, and the empty area will be filled with a duplicate of the original image.

The Styles, Effects, and Filter Panels

The Panel Effects

The Effects panel allows you to apply effects to images in a single location. Regardless of whether you are in Quick or Advanced mode, the Effects panel is always at the top. These are the pictures or effects that you can alter or add to a photo. There are usually a number of alternatives available to you, each with its own subcategories. Three effect kinds are available: Classic, Artistic, and Color Match.

Concerning photo effects

You may easily alter the appearance of your images by applying effects to them. From the Effects box, you may choose a segment like Panels, Faded Photo, Monotone Color, Textures, or Vintage Photo.

Using a frame

The margins of a layer or a portion of a layer may have various effects applied to it. To easily add to or modify the content, you can also create a drop zone using a frame.

Visual Effects

You may apply effects to a duplicate of a selected layer. When you apply the Blizzard effect to a photograph, it seems as if snow is falling. When the Neon Glow effect is applied, the image seems to be a brilliant neon sign. You may reduce the clarity and intensity of a photograph's colors by using picture effects like Oil Pastel or Soft Focus. Although you may be required to flatten the levels first, you may also blend image effects.

Textures

Include a variety of materials in a photograph. You may use any existing or newly created pattern as a backdrop for any image. To organize layers and create visually appealing and captivating images, you may use opacity and other layer techniques.

Note: Many image effects make use of filters with altered settings.

Utilizing an effect

Creative effects

You may apply effects to your photos to make them resemble well-known pieces of art or prominent art movements with just one click. Changing the appearance of your picture to get the desired effect is simple. You may apply lovely artistic effects to everything or some of it. It is possible to utilize visual effects in both the Quick and Advanced modes. **Do the following to add an artistic impact to your image:**

- Click Open to upload a photo of your choosing in either Quick mode or Advanced mode.
- To choose from a variety of artistic effects, click Effects & Artistics on the right side.
- You may apply any kind of creative effect to your image.

- **Take these actions:**
  - ➢ Describe intensity.
  - ➢ Selecting "Keep original photo colors" will preserve the picture's true hues.
  - ➢ The topic and/or backdrop of the picture may have their creative influence removed.
  - ➢ Select "Advanced" to alter the composition of the image or specific portions of it. You may choose portions of the image that you want to recompose by cutting them off in the Tool Options menu. You may also set the threshold and size.
- **Select File > Save As to save the image. Select File > Share to post it on social media.**

Traditional Effects

To improve the appearance of your images, use Photoshop Elements' Classic effects. You may choose your favorite among the 11 Classic effects available in the Quick and Advanced modes.
To add a classic touch to your photo, follow these steps:
- Launch Photoshop Elements and open an image.
- To choose from 11 traditional effects in Quick mode, select Effects > traditional. More than 30 vintage effects are available if you choose Effects > vintage in Advanced mode.
- Choose a classic effect that you like, and then apply it to your image.
- Select "Advanced" to reorganize the image or portions of it. You may conceal portions of the image that you want to recompose using the Brush tool under Tool Options. It is also possible to customize size and opacity.
- Select File > Save As to save the image. Select File > Share to post it on social media.

Note: Click the "Reset" button in the top right corner of the screen to remove all of the effects.

Effects of Color Match

You may use own photo or one of the pre-installed themes. Sharpness, color, and brightness may all be improved. You may experiment with the Color Match effect using the Quick and Advanced modes.

Use Quick mode to apply the Color Match effect

- To open a photo to which you want to apply an effect, either click the Open button or choose File > Open.
- In the Effects panel, choose Color Match and select one of the preset options.

Note: Because layers aren't created, if you apply a preset to the primary image, the effect from another preset will replace it. Additionally, Color Match effects cannot be used simultaneously.

There are two methods by which you may stack one configuration on top of another:

- Use the first preset's outcome as an input picture for the subsequent one, saving it.
- In Quick mode, use the first preset; then switch to Advanced mode. In Advanced mode, use the image you obtained in Quick mode as an input and choose the desired setting.

A. You may further alter your image's saturation, hue, and brightness to suit your preferences.

Note: You may reverse your changes by clicking the Undo button. You may redo them by clicking the Redo button.

B. Select File > Save As to save the image. Click Share to post it on social media.

Use the advanced mode to apply the Color Match effect

- To open an image to which you want to apply an effect, either click the Open button or choose File > Open.
- Press the "Advanced" button.
- By clicking the "Import photo" option in the Advanced mode, you may utilize your photo as a Custom preset. Additionally, you may choose from pre-made settings.

Note: You may utilize a custom option when the app is active since it is retained for the duration of the launch session. When you restart the application, it removes it to make room on the hard disk. Only the most recently used Custom preset will be retained and utilized for the remainder of the launch session, even if you load the Custom preset more than once. The previous Custom configuration will be replaced with the new one if you load a fresh one every time.

✦ You may adjust your picture's saturation, hue, and brightness more if necessary.

Note: You may choose File > Save As to save the image or File > Share to post it to social media.

Enhance Favorites with visuals or effects

Put a photo or effect in the Favorites area of the Effects panel so you can locate it easily later. To add an image to your favorites, right-click on it in the Graphics or Effects panel and choose "Add to Favorites."

The Panel Styles

Like the effects in the previous two panels, many of the effects in Styles are vintage versions of effects included with Photoshop Elements. Drop Shadows, Bevels, Image Effects, and Photographic Effects are all available here. Additionally, there are subheadings for Inner Glows, Inner Shadows, Outer Glows, Strokes, Patterns, Visibility, Wow Chrome, Wow Neon, and Wow Plastic. Some of these things can be used on images, but it works better on text layers. They may also be used to create visual art or web pages for extra effects.

The panel for graphics

The Graphics panel allows you to add text styles, theme embellishments, and artwork to your images in one location. Simply choose Window > Graphics to see the Graphics section. There are several tools in the Graphics panel's following sections that might assist you improve your images. You may choose from a variety of items, including text, forms, images, backdrops, and frames. Each tab has a drop-down menu where you may choose the ideal frames, backdrops, images, forms, or text to duplicate. Little previews of the artwork or effects that may be added to or altered on a photo can be found there. There are usually a number of alternatives available to you, each with its own subcategories.

Enhance a picture using stylistic forms or graphics

The image that existed before you added the shape or image remains unchanged. The image or form is a new layer.

- In the Graphics box, choose a group (such as "By Event" or "By Activity") and a subcategory (such as "Baby" or "Cooking").
- In the toolbox, choose a color for the form.
- **Choose one of the following actions to take:**
  - ➢ Click a thumbnail twice.
  - ➢ Drag the image to the thumbnail.
- To move or resize the image or form, use the Move tool.

Give a photograph a creative backdrop

A picture's existing layer is altered when an artistic backdrop is added. As an example, you might apply a layer between your family and a kitchen backdrop using the selection tools.
After that, you may go from the kitchen to the outdoors as the backdrop.

- Select the backdrop layer and select Layer > Duplicate Layer if it is the only layer in your image. After giving it a name, choose OK.
- From the Layers panel, choose the Background layer.
- In the Graphics panel, choose Backgrounds from the drop-down menu.
- **You ought to perform one of the following:**
  - ➢ Click a thumbnail twice.
  - ➢ Drag the picture to the thumbnail.

Give a picture a frame or a theme

You may add a theme or a frame to a photo project. Frames provide a gray, empty area for the image. Drag an image to the Photo Bin after selecting it.

- Select Frames from the drop-down menu in the Graphics box.
- **Select one of these:**
  - ➢ Select a thumbnail, and then select "Apply."
  - ➢ You must double-click on a thumbnail.
- Transfer the image to the unused backdrop
- Drag the desired image from the Photo Bin.
- Move the slider to adjust the picture's size in the frame or theme border, then click the Commit or Cancel button to save the changes.
- To save the adjustment, center the image using the Move tool and then click the Commit or Cancel button.

Utilizing Overlays and Textures

Using textures and overlays in Adobe Photoshop Elements allows you to add visual appeal, depth, and dimension to your images. With these tools, you may also apply effects to your images or designs, which can transform a plain image into something more captivating and lively. Let's examine how to use Photoshop Elements' textures and overlays.

Comprehending Textures

You may add textures to your photos to alter their appearance or feel. They might be gentle clouds, grunge patterns, wood grain, or concrete. Adding a texture may give your picture an aged, worn-out, or creative appearance, depending on the texture you choose and how you mix it with the original image.

How to Use Photoshop Elements to Add Texture

- **Import the Texture:** To begin, locate and import the texture file you want to utilize. Some sites provide free or paid photos, or you may create your own texture.
- To apply the texture to a new layer, first open Photoshop Elements and choose the primary image. After that, choose the texture file by going to File > Place. The texture will then appear as a new layer above your image.
- **Resize and Position:** You may adjust the wallpaper's size and position to suit your image.
- **Blend the Texture:** When adding a texture, it's crucial to have it blend in with the original picture. To do this, choose the Blending Mode option from the Layers panel. Try experimenting with other settings, such as Overlay, Soft Light, or Multiply, to see how the texture affects your image. The default option is "Normal." The way the texture blends with the layers underneath it varies with each setting.
- **Modify Opacity:** You may also adjust the Opacity slider to lessen the intensity of the pattern if it's too strong.
- **Masking and Erasing:** To limit the texture's impact to certain areas of your picture, use a layer mask. This enables you to use a black brush to "paint away" portions of the texture while preserving other areas of the picture. This is a fantastic method for adding textures to borders or backgrounds without changing the topic.

Textures' Typical Applications

- **Grunge and Vintage Effects:** Adding worn-out or rough backdrops to pictures may give them an aged, gritty appearance. This is commonly done to make images seem old or distressed.
- **Adding Depth:** To give flat images a more realistic appearance or depth, include soft textures like clouds or fabric patterns.
- **Creative Art:** To create odd or mixed-media pieces, artists often use many layers of textures.

Using Overlays

You may add images or effects to your photo as overlays. They are often used to produce visual effects like bokeh, snow, sparkles, and light leaks. Overlays may alter an image's mood without altering the original by adding these supplementary components.

How to Use Photoshop Elements to Apply an Overlay

- **Select an Overlay:** Similar to graphics, overlays may be created or downloaded. Overlays of light flares, fog, rain, and other weather phenomena are often used.
- **Place the Overlay:** Just as with textures, choose an overlay and then select File > Place to place it over your image.
- **Resize and Position:** To make the overlay fit the image; you may adjust its size and placement.
- **Blend the Overlay:** To simply make the overlay blend in with your image, use the Blending Modes in the Layers box. Try using the Screen or Overlay modes for light-based overlays.
- **Use Layer Masks:** You may use a layer mask to tone down or eliminate areas of the overlay that are too intense.
- **Fine-Tune:** Depending on the look you desire, you may adjust the overlay effect's brightness or use filters to make it softer or sharper.

Typical Applications for Overlays

- **Light Leaks and Flares:** To create a bright, sunny mood in your images, use light leaks and lens flare layers.
- **Bokeh Effects:** Often used to create a soft, enchanting backdrop for photographs or wedding photos, bokeh overlays are light orbs that are out of focus.
- **Seasonal Effects:** To add atmosphere to a scene, adding snow, rain, or falling leaves on top of a photograph is a popular approach to enhance seasonal images.

Blending Overlays and Textures

One of the most inventive methods to enhance a picture is to combine overlays and textures. To give your subject a warm, dramatic appearance, you might, for instance, apply a light flare overlay after applying a grunge texture to the backdrop to make the image seem aged and rugged. By adjusting the blend modes, opacity, and masking, you may get a highly distinctive and creative effect.

Extra Advice for Using Textures and Overlays

Try Various Layers: To create more intricate effects, don't be scared to layer various overlays and textures on top of one another. **You may manipulate which layers appear and how they interact with one another by using masks and blending modes.**

- **Use High-Resolution Files:** To prevent pixelation, particularly on larger images, all of your textures and graphics should be high-resolution.
- **Color Adjustments:** Use Hue/Saturation adjustments to alter the color tones of textures and overlays that don't match your image.

Producing Effects of Double Exposure

- **Select the first exposure:** Open your first photo and choose the Quick option to adjust the exposure. After that, choose Fun Edits under the Guided tab. You must choose Double Exposure here. Click and hold the left mouse button on the object you want to select with the Quick tool, and then move it around until it is in position. If the backdrop is bright and the subject is dark, it will look its finest.

- **Select a second exposure:** There are now two alternatives available to you. Click "Import a photo" to begin by selecting a photograph to use as your second exposure from the hard disk of your computer. A subject with a lot of contrast against a bright or white backdrop will provide the greatest results, just as in your first image.

↓ **Set up a second exposure:** As you can see, the second exposure only appears where we selected in the first phase. By clicking and dragging the corners of the Move Tool, you may adjust the size and position of this second image until you're satisfied.

➢ **Make use of an Elements exposure:** Another option is to utilize one of Elements' pre-existing photos for your second exposure. The cloud is ideal for our image of the bird. You may use the Intensity tool to adjust the strength of the double exposure effect.

↓ **Include a color effect:** A color treatment may be applied on top of the double exposure after you are happy with it. You may click through the images in the Effects tab to choose a desired image, and you can adjust the Intensity using the slider. Some effects may seem too "Instagrammy," so you may want to exercise caution!

↓ **Output and Crop:** Click "Next," and you may continue editing in Advanced Mode. You may use the Crop tool to adjust the frame of your image if necessary. When you're finished, click Layer > Flatten Image and save the image.

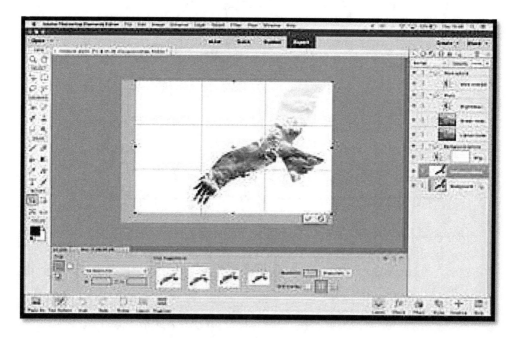

CHAPTER TWELVE
LAYER AND LAYER MASKS UNDERSTANDING

Layers: What Are They?

Layers are among Adobe Photoshop Elements' most crucial tools for producing, modifying, and working with images. Think of layers as a stack of transparent sheets. Each layer can hold different components of your image, such as text, shapes, or images. You can work on different sections of this structure without affecting the others. You have more autonomy and control over the adjustments you make as a result. For example, when creating a poster, you may have a background layer, a text layer, and a third layer for any additional images. Layers make it simple to manage these distinct elements by allowing you to move them around, conceal or reveal them, and apply various effects to each one.

Important Features of Layers

- **Non-Destructive Editing:** By using layers, you can make changes without permanently altering the original image. This allows you to experiment with various effects, filters, and adjustments. It is possible to switch between layers, alter their visibility, and blend them in different ways.
- **Layer Order:** The proper order of the layers is essential. The layer at the top of the panel will appear before the other layers. In the Layers panel, you can move layers around by dragging them up or down.
- **Blending Modes:** Layers may interact with one other using blending mode. These modes regulate how the colors of one layer merge with those of the one below it. A layer may be made darker with the "Multiply" mode and lighter with the "Screen" option, for example.
- **Opacity:** You can change how transparent a layer is by moving the opacity slider that comes with it. You may use this to generate an effect that seems like a ghost or to diminish the impact of a specified portion of your picture.

Layer masks: what are they?

There is another key feature in Photoshop Elements called a layer mask. It works with layers to provide you even greater freedom over editing. You may conceal or display elements of a layer without harming the layer itself using a layer mask. You may display or conceal sections of a layer without deleting any information. It's sort of like painting on transparency. A thumbnail related to the layer depicts what a layer mask looks like. If you use a layer mask, the color black conceals sections of the layer, while the color white displays them. Several grayscale hues may be combined to create semi-transparency, which is helpful for creating delicate blends or fades.

The Operation of Layer Masks

- To create a Layer Mask, click the Add Layer Mask button at the bottom of the Layers panel after selecting the layer you want to work on. This will apply a mask to the chosen layer. This places a white box (the mask) next to the picture of the layer to demonstrate that the complete layer can be viewed. You may now "paint" using the brush tool anything you wish to reveal (white) or conceal (black).
- **Non-Destructive Editing:** Similar to layers, masks allow you to make changes to a picture without destroying it. Parts of the layer may be hidden rather than removed. You may "paint" the concealed areas back into view by switching the mask's color from black to white if you decide to change your mind later.
- **Fine Editing Control:** Layer masks are an excellent tool for fine-tuning your image modifications. For example, a layer mask allows you to conceal the areas you don't want without erasing them entirely if you want to remove the backdrop from a picture. If you make a mistake, you may return to the original portions of the picture by painting over the masked region.

Real-World Applications for Layers and Layer Masks

- **Photo Compositing:** Photo compositing is the process of combining multiple images into one. For this, layers and masks are crucial. Each image can be placed on its own layer, and they can be smoothly blended using masks. This is helpful for creating effects like background changes and double exposure.
- **Local Adjustments:** You may create an adjustment layer and remove the portions of an image that you don't want to modify if you simply want to make certain changes, such as brightening the sky without altering the rest of the image.
- **Creating Complex Text Effects:** Text may be creatively treated using layers and masks to give it gradients or textures, for example. Masks allow you to adjust the amount of affect that is applied to the text.

Examining some of Layers' foundational concepts

- **Layers #1:** Click the Layer menu at the top of the screen, and then choose Duplicate Layer to create a duplicate of a layer. In the panel that displays the duplicate layer (which is situated in the center of the picture above), click OK. It should become second nature to name your layers. When you return to the task later, this will assist you locate them. Two layers are now identical to one another in the Layer panel (right above). The layer that is being utilized is the one that is shown in blue. This implies that any modifications you make to this file, such as altering the color or brightness, will only affect this layer and not the one behind it. After duplicating a layer, you just place a duplicate over the original picture, so the main screen won't change. This is because the copy is the same as the original, so you will not notice any changes. The duplicated layer will always be put on top of the original layer. This duplicated layer is called the

Background layer. A tiny padlock icon appears to the right of the Background layer's name, which is indicated by an arrow. This signifies that portion of the layer is locked and can't be altered or shrunk. To remove the padlock, just click the symbol once; it will immediately become Layer 0 and be ready to be reinstalled.

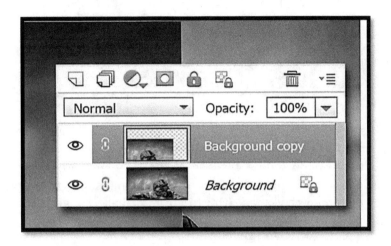

+ **Layers #2:** If you copy a layer and then use the Move Tool to move it, you will be able to see the layer behind it. You will see that the two photographs are similar when you look at both the main screen and the thumbnail for this layer. So you can see this detail, I shifted this layer down and to the left a bit. We can see what is underneath that section of the file because the picture that has been moved (in the Layer panel) has a checkerboard pattern surrounding it. Furthermore, as openness is a crucial component of the construction process, it will be mentioned often. I should start by examining the many components of layers and how to utilize them to express creativity. Regardless of the size, quality, or color style of the internal image, it occupies a single layer. In most cases, it is made up of pixels. It will be made up of components called vectors whether it is a textual or graphic representation.

+ **Layers #3:** In addition to the tiny thumbnail that appears in the Layer panel, the active layer would change to a black-and-white version if I chose the Convert to Black and White option from the Enhance drop-down menu and clicked OK (I don't need to choose a black-and-white style). Although the Convert to Black and White option displays the picture as being in black and white, the color layer is opaque, therefore we are unable to see what is happening in the event stack. Clicking the little eye symbol to the left of the thumbnail in the current layer will display the black-and-white version. The top layer will become undetectable as a result. When I switch the visibility of that layer "off," we can see the freshly converted black-and-white version of the information in the layer underneath it. The layer is not visible if a red line appears over the eye symbol. Although it might be challenging to remember which layer you are working on, you should be able to do so as long as you pay attention to the Layer panel.

- **Layer #4:** Using the Transform tool (Ctrl/Cmd + T), I may push one of the square sides of the image inward to reduce the size of the color layer. There will be less color on the layer after this. As you reduce the size of the layer, the previous color version will appear underneath the smaller one. Elements prompts you to click the red symbol (cancel) or the green checkmark (OK) to affirm or halt changes you make to a layer. After that, you'll be free to continue evolving.

- **Layer #5:** A text layer is created when words are added to a file. This is composed of vectors rather than pictures. A vector layer is a mathematical formula that can be enlarged to any dimension without losing quality since it is only an algorithm. In contrast, a pixel-based layer can only be expanded so far before quality begins to degrade. This is the primary distinction between a vector layer and a pixel layer. When you modify the size of an image on a layer, elements employ sophisticated interpolation or resampling techniques to determine how many pixels are required to make the image larger or how to remove pixels to make it smaller. This allows you to adjust the image's size. But in order to prevent obvious pixilation, it requires a great deal of dithering, which softens the pixel boundaries and softens the scaled picture that results.

- **Layers #6:** You will discover that adding text is a reasonably simple procedure after experimenting with layers for some time. With this knowledge, you may begin a variety of creative text-based tasks, such as creating flyers, posters, and even business cards. To illustrate how tough the sport is, Myriad Pro, which seemed to be a typical font, was replaced with one that was a little rougher. I used the red SoulMission typeface after I finished creating the drop shadow, which was taken from the Styles section. You may discover other graphic layers in Elements. These layers allow you to create your own shapes and apply them to any text. These may be text boxes, copyright stamps, or other images, among other things. Like the other pixel-based layers, the text layer may be altered independently of the rest of the picture. If you have terrible typing habits like I do, this tool is fantastic since it allows you to alter text from inside the picture.

+ **Layer #7:** Text may be made to stand out from the image's surface by using drop shadows. A picture like this gains depth and readability when text is superimposed on top of it. A picture with a lot going on might be challenging to interpret. Selecting the appropriate font is another crucial factor that influences the outcome of any video production that contains text. Lack of knowledge about font styles (bold, italic), font choices, and point sizes may make or ruin a project. If you want the font to be the only thing you can read, you may also put text boxes below the text. Alternatively, you may reduce the opaqueness of the text box to allow some of the images to pass through. This will prevent the text box from appearing as a solid color block on the picture.

The Panel Layers

The Layer panel is located on the right side of the main window while you are in Advanced Edit mode. It has many practical tools. These buttons run along the top of the panel. **These are them, left to right:**

+ **Create a New Layer (highlighted in red):** To add a new layer to your document, please click the button. Since it is blank, the backdrop seems clear, which is why it is checkered.

+ **Create a New Group:** If you have a large number of layers, you may wish to condense the Layer panel by putting comparable layers into a folder named "Group." Grouped layers are able to move, modify, and conceal themselves as one cohesive unit.

- To change a layer without altering the source file, create a new fill or adjustment layer. The term "non-destructive" refers to the fact that the target layer's images remain unchanged. Adjustment layers come with a mask that you may utilize if you simply want to change certain areas of the target layer. This is shown in the white picture.
- **Add a Layer Mask:** Masks provide you far more flexibility when it comes to altering distinct areas of a layer. You may use a black-and-white tool to reveal or conceal portions of the image.

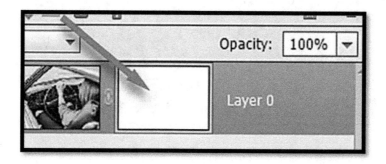

- To lock every pixel, tap the "Lock All Pixels" green arrow. This will prevent you from altering the layers further.
- **Lock Transparency (yellow arrow):** This will safeguard you from mistakenly losing the sections of the document that you can see, as when you paint over them.
- Eliminate the clutter by deleting the layer (the red arrow). This part looks like it's pretty clear. In the menu that shows up when you right-click on a layer, you may also pick "Delete Layer."

Opacity of layers

The Opacity tool allows you to adjust a layer's transparency or opacity. Making the top layer less opaque allows you to mix layers. If a layer has a low viewing number, you can see what's underneath it. If you need to move the top layer directly on top of an item in the layer behind it, this might be helpful. Once the layer is in the proper location, you may continue tweaking and make it completely see-through once again. In this instance, I have reduced the MAGAZINE text layer by 50%. Keeping the various components on distinct levels is the best method to create this type of effect. If you don't, Classic Car will also disappear, making it useless.

Layers merging

If you right-click the little icon to the right of the trash can, you can access to the same options and buttons on the Layer panel. This will bring up a menu at the top of the screen that resembles the Layer menu. It offers the same options. Merging two levels into a single active layer is one option. Note: You won't be able to return to those levels once you save the project as a Photoshop file and shut it. Merge Visible, on the other hand, is a bit different since it creates a single layer from all of the visible layers. Because it merges all the layers into a single layer, the Flatten Image command is superior. Keep an eye on the Layer panel if you wish to save a Photoshop project with multiple layers as a JPEG file. After automatically flattening the layers and saving the file as a JPEG, Elements will flatten everything once again when it returns to its multi-layered.psd format. This will offer you both the original .psd file and a.jpg file that has been trimmed down.

Layers of Adjustment

The operation of a ghost layer is similar to that of an adjustment layer. With this tool, the tone of a typical image may be altered without causing any damage. "Non-destructive" makes this very evident. Some individuals make excessive, frequent, or inadequate edits to files, particularly JPEG images, which might damage the files. If it's not a RAW file, which is always a duplicate of the original, the image will deteriorate with time. Furthermore, while this assertion that data are not destroyed sounds fantastic, it is difficult to demonstrate in practice since there are methods of altering files that can do harm. However, for many photographers, the ability to utilize an adjustment layer as a mask is one of its finest features. Photoshop Elements has a tool called a mask that may be used to pick out certain regions of a picture and reduce the impact of color or other changes. Without altering anything else, you may make some areas of an image brighter, darker, more saturated, or less saturated. Additionally, creating a mask is a really easy feature. You may apply an Adjustment Layer to any image by clicking on the button at the top of the Layers menu or the Layers menu itself, which is located at the top of the main screen.

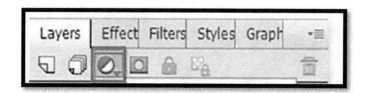

From the menu, you may choose Adjustment Layer effects such as Pattern, Levels, Hue/Saturation, Brightness/Contrast, Gradient Map, Photo Filter, Invert, Threshold, and Posterize. You can see the well-known Levels curve in the center of the screen since I choose the Levels Adjustment Layer. Only the areas of the scene that need additional contrast or brightness should be altered when adjusting the levels. If the remainder seems too bright or too dark, that's OK. To the right of the Levels button is the mask for the Adjustment Layer. I boosted the scene's contrast by adjusting the two tiny buttons on each side of the tone histogram.

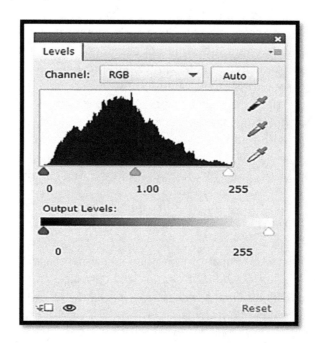

You may either utilize the white mask to make the tone changes appear just in certain areas of the image, or you can save the Adjustment Layer as a TIFF or PSD file and leave it alone.

Masking of Adjustment Layers

- As soon as you click on the white square that symbolizes the layer mask, it will be selected. To indicate that the white mask square is now the active portion of the Adjustment Layer, a light blue line will appear around it. Before you may "paint" into the area of the layer that allows you to make modifications, Element will inform you that

136

this layer has to be smoothed out. The layer should be laid flat. To view the mask, click the white button after selecting "Cancel."

- Select the Brush tool from the Tool Bar. To do this, click the brush symbol in the Draw line of the Tool Bar or press B. Verify that the brush tip you selected—hard, soft, large, or small—is appropriate for the task.

- Press D for the standard color selection. This makes the paint white in the center and black in the background. You will only receive black paint if you do this. To change black to white, use the X key. To turn it back to black, press X once again.

- You can paint directly on the main screen image if you choose the white mask icon. Keep in mind that painting black on top of the white mask will remove the impact that the Levels modification had on the brightness and contrast. You can notice it when the mask is dark. You can see your black brush strokes in the picture if you look closely. When you paint, the primary scene doesn't really alter.

- You may paint over the black paint on that area of the mask to make it see-through again after painting it black by mistake. Press the X key to change black to white. To get the tone exactly perfect or in the proper position, you may adjust it as many times as you want. You may continue to change it.

The enhanced image, which has increased contrast in certain places, namely along the coastline, is on the bottom right, while the original image is on the left.

Masking layers

Layer masking allows you to make significant adjustments to extremely precise areas of any image. Among the most helpful features of any picture editor is this one. Once it is set up, it is simple to modify as you see fit. First, a general adjustment is made using an editing program such as Levels. You can look through the layer and view the image as it was before by adding black to the mask while it is still active. By sketching white on the mask, you may solidify it. This will overlay the modified image over the original. Even if you intended for the mask to remain improved, if you make a mistake and paint over anything in the mask, that portion of the image returns to its original state. This approach excels in that situation. Press the X key to turn the white background black. When white paint is applied to black paper, the error is instantly corrected.

This back-and-forth stopping is a really helpful editing technique since it may be used again.

- Layer masks are easy to set up. Launch a picture. You may witness wooden houses that are more than a century old in this section of Kyoto's old town. It was a boring day, therefore the photo turned out the same. Careful assistance is required. Duplicate the layer. Although this step is optional, I always work on (or change) a duplicate of the original layer and leave it alone. By clicking the eye symbol and disabling the editing layer, I can easily return to the original inside the same file.

- Verify again that the cloned layer at the top is the current layer (highlighted in blue) and that you can see the Layer panel clearly. On top of that layer is a row of buttons that are solely used for layer switching. The button that I like to examine is called "Add a Layer Mask". A white thumbnail will display to the right of the photo image for that layer when you click this. You have just made your very own Layer Mask. At this point, a white Layer Mask doesn't change the picture because it's see-through.
- Modify the layer's tone. To demonstrate the usage of Levels (Ctrl/Cmd + L), let's brighten the image. Make sure you choose the picture thumbnail rather than the cover thumbnail before proceeding. Double-clicking the picture will select it and create a light blue outline around it. The hue and/or brightness of the image may be altered. I can only see the updated version on the screen since I can still see through the white mask. Some portions seem excellent and sections that could be overly bright.

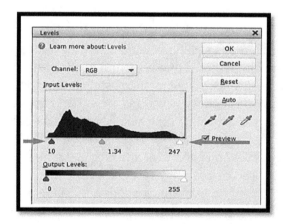

- When you click on the white layer image, light blue lines will appear around its edges. Make sure it's the actual paintbrush and not the Color Replacement or Impressionist brushes before selecting it. Next, choose black using the Color Picker, which consists of two tiny color squares located beneath "Modify" at the toolbar's bottom. Changing the background color to black and the normal center color to white can be accomplished quickly by pressing the D key. Then hit the X key. This gives you black paint by making the middle color blend in with the background.
- Paint over the desired area to restore the image to its original brightness. As you paint on the image (actually on the mask) using a black paintbrush, you can see that the contrast and brightness have returned to their previous levels. When you release the mouse, the black paint appears in the mask thumbnail rather than the main image.
- The mask's masking state changes when you stop drawing and release the mouse. This feature will therefore continuously change as you create your mask, allowing you to quickly assess how well it conceals everything.

To improve this technique even further, remember that you can alter the brush's size, shape, density, and softness. This implies that a photographer or artist can make very minor adjustments to an image's appearance. Finally, you can alter the color or tone of the blocked areas without using Levels on the covered layer. Any tool that changes tone can be used. To bring off the atmosphere of these ancient Japanese residences, I utilized Hue/Saturation to make the colors on the wooden walls stand out more. This masking example is quite simple, but I hope that by demonstrating how it works, you will have an understanding of how powerful this approach can be.

Layer Masks: Adding Transparency

- **The Layer Can Be Duplicated (Optional):** Making a duplicate of the layer you want to work with is typically a smart idea in order to safeguard the original. Once the layer has been selected in the Layers panel, right-click on it and chooses "Duplicate Layer."
- **Incorporate a Layer Mask:** With the layer selected, click the "Layer Mask" button at the bottom of the Layers panel. A circle appears in the center of what seems to be a square. In the Layers panel, a white layer mask picture will show up next to your layer as a result.
- **Click on the Brush Tool:** Go to the toolbox and choose the Brush Tool. You may use the "B" key on your keyboard to pick it fast.
- **Adjust Brush Settings:** Make sure the layer mask thumbnail is selected and the foreground color is set to black in the Layers panel. You may adjust the brush size, density, and hardness to your liking using the settings at the top of the screen.
- **Apply paint to the layer mask:** After setting the Brush Tool to black, choose the layer mask. Next, apply paint to the areas that you want to be transparent. Black painting on the layer mask allows you to see through those areas to the layers below.
- **Changing the foreground colors is optional:** To remove your brush strokes or view what you've concealed, set the color of the foreground to white. If you paint white on the layer mask, the locations you've concealed will show up.

- **Adapt Flow and Opacity (Optional):** You may modify the Brush Tool's opacity and flow to change how see-through the blocked regions are. A lower visibility setting will cause the shift to occur more slowly, while a higher visibility setting will cause it to occur more rapidly.
- **Fine-tune and Save:** Continue sketching in black and white on the layer mask until the desired transparency is achieved. Remember that the actual picture is not altered; you are only concealing or exposing certain areas of the layer.

Make non-square graphics

If you wish to create non-square pictures with Photoshop Elements, you may either adjust the canvas's size or utilize layers and shapes to get the desired form. **You may accomplish it in the following ways:**

- **Adjusting Canvas Size:**
  - **Launch an Existing Image or Create a New File:**
    - ✓ Launch Photoshop Elements and choose to open an existing file or create a new one.
  - **Resize the Canvas:**
    - ✓ To adjust the canvas size, click Image, then Resize.
    - ✓ Adjust the height and width of your non-square picture to your preferred values. Be careful not to tick the "Constrain Proportions" option if you want to alter the aspect ratio.
    - ✓ To position your present content into the new canvas area, you may also pick the anchor point.
  - **Design or Fill the Extended Canvas:**
    - ✓ You may use tools like the Brush Tool and the Shape Tool, or you can import other photos or graphics, to fill the enlarged area with a color, a gradient, or other design components.
- **Making Use of Layers and Shapes:**
  - **Make a New Layer:**
    - ✓ Create a new file or open an existing one in Photoshop Elements.
    - ✓ To create a non-square shape that resembles the desired image, use the Shape Tool (such as Rectangle or Ellipse). You may access the Shape Tool from the menu.
  - **Change and Adjust the Shape:**
    - ✓ To alter the shape's size, location, and other attributes, uses the choices in the Tool choices bar at the top.
    - ✓ Use several forms and organize them together by creating distinct layers for each shape to generate complicated visuals that aren't square.
  - **Add Design Elements:**
    - ✓ Using additional layers, you may overlay or insert text, photos, or other design components inside the shapes to create the desired image.
  - **Adjust and Set Up Layers:**

✓ To create the style you desire, utilize the Layers panel to move your shapes and design components around adjust their size, or apply blending selections.

Transformations: A Picture within a Picture

Another wonderful approach to understand how layers operate in Photoshop Elements is to construct a poster using more than one photo. **You can modify the sizes of the photographs in a file and shift them about so they sit next to one other instead of on top of each other.**

+ **Step 1:** Open the photographs you wish to utilize in the project. Keep in mind that their photos are located in the lower left corner of the Photo Bin.

+ **Step 2:** Select File > New > Blank File to create a new document the size of your print.

+ **Step 3:** Once the "New" box pops up, you can fill in the document's base size as well as its height and width. You may also easily pick one of the common document sizes from the Document Type drop-down box. A4, A3, US letter, HD video, and others are among them. Set the quality to 200 or 300 dpi if you want to print the picture. The white new Background Layer will show up on the screen when you click OK.

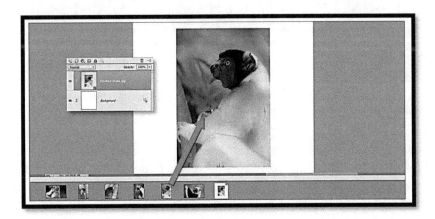

+ **Step 4:** While the white new document is on the main screen, drag and drop an image clip from the Photo Bin onto the main image. The white paper will be topped with this. When you're finished, ensure sure your image is now on a new layer above the white backdrop by checking the Layer box. The image may be saved as a TIFF (.tif) or Photoshop (.psd) file. Remember that JPEGs cannot include layers, masks, or selections.

+ **Step 5:** Repeat the process with the additional images you wish to utilize for the poster. Verify that the new image appears in the Layer box each time you add it to your main document. A picture will always obscure the previous one when it is copied into the master document. Don't worry, however; we're going to rearrange everything to improve the design. Proceed to the next tag and save your work.

+ **Step 6:** Using a transformation is the simplest way to alter the size of anything on a single layer. This holds true regardless of whether the object is made of vectors or pixels. Select Image > Transform > Free Transform to get started. You may also use the Move tool by clicking and dragging the area of the image you want to modify, or by pressing Ctrl or Cmd + T. When you select this, Adobe's "corner handles" grid will appear across that single picture. The image will become smaller the appropriate direction if you click, hold, and pull one edge in.

There is a handle in the center of each side. The picture will become smaller and crooked if you drag one of them. Avoid this. A green check mark will show up in the lower right corner of the image after it has been resized to better fit the screen. To confirm that you wish to alter the size in this instance, click it. Then, to halt and restart, click the red symbol.

➕ **Step 7:** Modify every other picture in the Photo Bin in the same way. Verify that they are all the appropriate size to match in the chosen style. When you alter a picture's size (making it larger or smaller), elements wait for your approval before proceeding. Although this is a positive quality, if you aren't careful, getting stuck and not knowing why can be annoying.

To confirm, click the green OK button or hit Enter on the keyboard. To halt the activity, click the red "No Entry" button or hit the "Esc" key. Most of the activities in this program may be undone by tapping these keys. Also, don't forget that one of the nicest things about working with layers is that you can still alter each element of the text independently after it is on its layer. Having a person who changes their mind a lot will find this extremely beneficial.

➕ **Step 8:** To add text, double-check the Layer panel by selecting the Horizontal Type tool from the Tool Bar or by using the T key. Then, click once inside the document to create a new text layer. You will notice that the type placement point blinks right where you clicked in the image. As soon as you begin typing, the program is likely to remember the font and point size you last chose using the Type tool.

To use the Type tool, click on the text once. This will allow you to type a message. Adding text to any image is simple with one of the Graphics panel's text styles. The View menu should not be used. Instead, practice using the edge lines by using the Grid. To access Preferences, press and hold Ctrl or Cmd + K. Next, set the line width to ten. It will be much simpler to use correctly because there will be fewer lines. The grid's color can also be changed. Keep in mind that the design and alignment tools are only visible on the screen; they do not print.

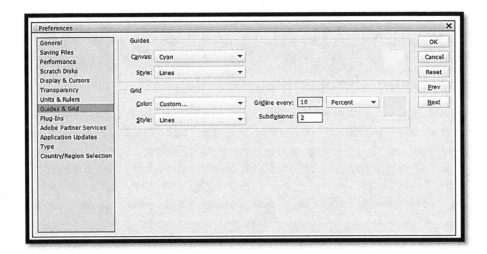

About smart objects

Be aware that an image becomes a Smart Object when you click and drag it from the Photo Bin into a new master document in the main edit window. You can also add a picture using the File>Place tool. Layers that don't alter anything are possible. You cannot adjust a pixel-based picture layer at will without endangering the pixels, in contrast. You can use masks and adjustment layers together. A Smart Object layer cannot be used to paint, avoid, burn, or clone pixels until it is converted to a conventional layer. The Simplify Layer function converts the layer's state from "smart" to "pixels." For many tasks, you have to convert a Smart Object back into a pixel-based image. Later, to accomplish this, right-click the image and choose Simplify Layer from the menu that displays. You will be alerted by Elements when this is required. This picture is a combination of the wrestler's image and the man's black-and-white shot. The smart layer is visible above the backdrop layer in the Layer panel. The "Smart Layer" symbol is located in the lower right corner.

You may drag the image corner handle in or out to adjust the picture's size. Every time you alter the image's dimensions or form, Elements adjusts the image's quality to match. This ensures that the quality of the image remains constant regardless of the distance.

Transformations: Correcting perspective

Most of the time, our images are more skewed since I capture them from ground level and aim the camera up at large structures. Some of the lines that travel up and down and left and right have to be modified so that the visual system can fit more information into a limited space. To prevent this sort of perspective distortion, shoot across from a tall structure from a high level. So, you won't have to move the camera as much, and the image should be crisper. **Nevertheless, we're back to street level and skewed perspectives since I can't do it very frequently.**

- Open the picture. As you can see, the wide-angle lens has screwed up the columns a lot, which I need to correct. The ceiling is quite lovely and is supported up by several stone columns.
- When I deal with photographs like these, I utilize the Grid tool (View>Grid) to get a clearer feel of what's vertical and what's not. If there are too many lines in the Grid, you may adjust their color by selecting Edit > Preferences or by pressing Ctrl/Cmd + K. This is the magical part. Image > Transform > Perspective is where you'll find the Transformation tool. The sides, or handles, of the Transformation tool appear along the boundaries of the frame. To launch the transformation tool, press Ctrl or Cmd + T. Then it will open in Free Transform mode, which you can see at the top of the new menu bar.

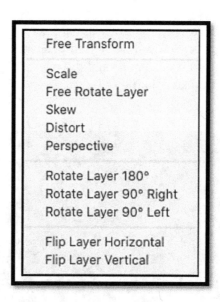

- Take hold of one of the upper corners and pull it out of the image. Keep in mind that the opposite direction of movement occurs when you pull out one corner. On the surface, you're enlarging the image's top. Verify the Grid to make sure everything is even.

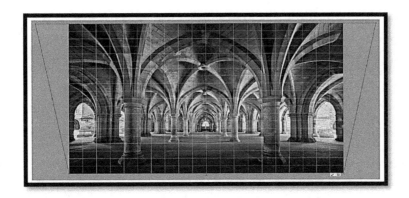

On paper, this method must seem like a dream because all those architectural shots that gave the building the appearance of falling backward can now be fixed. If the fix is fairly large, a significant portion of the original image may also be lost. The reason for this is that the edges will be pulled off. Once the building has been photographed, take a few steps back to reveal more of the surrounding area. When you use Photoshop Elements to edit the image in this manner, you will not lose as many important details.

- You can observe that when the top of the rectangular image is widened, the side of the image loses a few pixels. It seems less straight as a result of this as well. After saving the change by clicking OK or pressing Enter, I usually switch the Transform feature from Perspective to Scale and drag the top-center handle up to enlarge the image. This reduces the distortion and brings it closer to its initial size. More of the image will be lost if you do this, but that's to be expected as pixels are being altered! It's finished when you click OK.

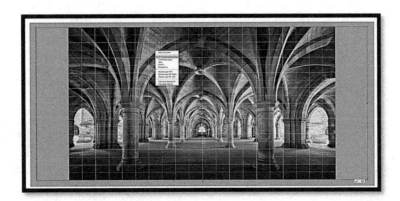

By right-clicking within the transformation box, you may see several modes. These are some of them:

- **Free Rotate Layer:** You may click and rotate the full picture or image layer using the Free Rotate Layer tool if you move the mouse to a corner.
- **Skew:** This mode twists objects in a fascinating manner. There is a mode where you can just click and drag the central handles to move them left or right. There is no mobility on

145

the sides. When structures appear like they are leaning more vertically, this option is the ideal one to utilize. The tower in Pisa, Italy, no longer needs to lean.

- **Distort:** The final Transformation mode is named "Distort." This is also the setting that shows when you click Ctrl or Cmd + T on your computer. I use this a lot when I produce photos, like when I make 3D text. If you grip and pull on a corner, this tool will bend the frame in the direction you aim it. This is a really helpful tool if the others don't work.

Using Warp Transformations to Produce a 3D Shadow

Although I've been using this portion of the Transform tool for a while, it was previously limited to Photoshop. Lastly, this function has been added to the list of Transform commands we looked at before (Image > Transform > Scale/Rotate/Skew/Distort/Perspective and now Warp modes).
Let's examine the use of this new Elements tool:

- I made a fresh, blank document and copied and pasted the picture in question. I then made the layer smaller than the base by using picture>Transform>Scale. I then duplicated Layer 1 to create two identical levels.

- After selecting Layer 1 to create the drop shadow layer, I used the Levels tool's Output Levels scale (Ctrl/Cmd + L) to shift the pin from the far right to the far left. The image goes dark.

- To give the impression that the drop shadow would land in those locations, I used the Move tool to move the shadow layer to the right and down. Additionally, I made 50% of the dark layer solid. The "shadow" can then be adjusted if it's too light or dark.

- Press Ctrl or Cmd + T to alter each layer's shape independently, giving the impression that they are in three dimensions. Do you notice the metal grid above the image? You may grab any portion of this grid to begin forming the pixels into the desired shape. I pulled the mesh's edges in and out using the knobs on the sides to bend them. Almost every image may be resized to suit any form. Press the Esc key to restart if you run into trouble.

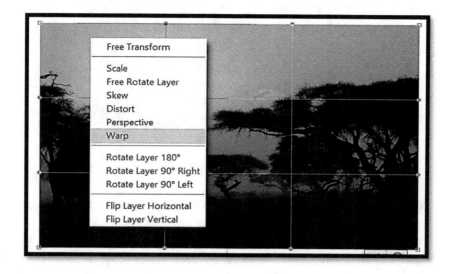

⊹ I must smooth out the shadow layer to give the drop shadow a more realistic appearance. To utilize the tool, choose Filter > Blur > Gaussian Blur. The subject needs to be less clear and lighter as it gets "higher" from the background. 9.8 squares worked for me this time. This and the strength of the layer may be adjusted at any moment.

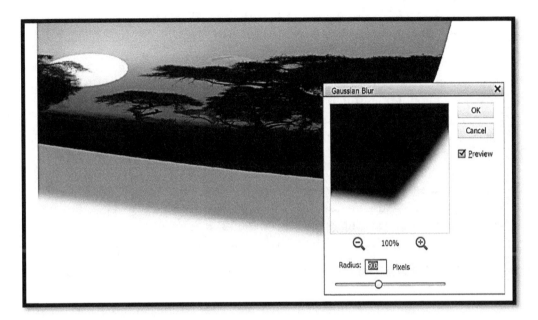

⊹ In the end, I reversed the top photo layer. This added to the 3D impact I was aiming for by intensifying the goofy appearance of the distorted shadow underneath the picture.

CHAPTER THIRTEEN

EXPLORING COLOR THEORY: THE USAGE

Using a Logical Process to Edit Your Photographs

- Resize, trim, and straighten your photos as needed.
- Once the photos are in the proper physical condition, adjust the lighting and ensure that the shadows, highlights, and midtones have a decent tonal range. This will display the maximum amount of information. Fixing minor color issues often just requires changing the lighting. Next, adjust the color balance if it doesn't.
- Remove any color casts and adjust the brightness as necessary.
- To correct any imperfections, use the retouching tools, such as the filters and healing tools.
- You may add enhancements or special effects if you'd like.
- If you think your picture needs more clarity and sharpness, sharpen it.

By following these steps and setting aside a few minutes of your time, you can make all of your photos ready for printing, posting, and sharing with loved ones.

Modifying the Lighting

You can adjust the lighting in Elements with a few basic manual tools if the auto tools I described didn't work or were too...automatic for you. You have greater control over the overall contrast and may emphasize features in the shadows, midtones, and highlights of your photos using the manual tools. Both the Advanced and Quick modes allow you to make any modifications to the lighting.

Using shadows and highlights to adjust the lighting

Using the Shadows/Highlights command, as shown on the left in the picture below, you may quickly and simply correct regions that are either too or too little exposed. This feature works particularly well for photos that were shot in strong overhead light or backlighting. In these pictures, the subject is usually obscured by shadows, either completely or partly.

To utilize the Shadows/Highlights adjustment, follow these steps:

- Check the Preview checkbox after choosing Enhance > Adjust Lighting > Shadows/Highlights in either Advanced or Quick mode. The preview instantly receives the default correction when the dialog box appears.
- If the default adjustment doesn't work, use the sliders (or enter a value) to vary the amount that your highlights (bright parts), midtones (middle-toned areas), and shadows (dark areas) are corrected. It is your responsibility to highlight the dark and bright areas of the picture. Add or subtract contrast in the areas of your image that are in the middle tones if it still seems like it needs improvement. You may choose only the portion of your picture that needs to be fixed before making any adjustments.
- Click OK to dismiss the text box and apply the change. Press the Alt (or Option on a Mac) key to restart. The Reset button will replace the Cancel button. To begin again, choose "Reset."

Contrast and Brightness Usage

If you choose to utilize the Brightness/Contrast command, just select the regions that need to be corrected, like Alcatraz in the example below. Once you have chosen, pick Enhance > Adjust Lighting > Brightness/Contrast.

Using levels to determine the appropriate contrast

The Levels command is all you need to do to alter an image's brightness, contrast, and even color. Compared to the other lighting and color adjustment dialog boxes, the Levels command dialog box is a little more complex, but it can be extremely simple to use if you understand how it works. You can see what Levels can accomplish if you utilize Auto Levels. You have far more control with the Levels command, its manual counterpart. While Brightness and Contrast only allow you to alter two fundamental values, Levels allows you to alter 256 distinct tones, ranging from bright to dark. Keep in mind that you may apply the Levels command to a specified region, a single layer, or the whole picture. The Levels command may also be used with an editing layer. If you're serious about picture editing, you should be able to utilize the Levels command.

Levels operate as follows:

- **In Advanced or Quick mode, choose Enhance, then Adjust Lighting, and lastly Levels.** I recommend using Advanced mode for this activity. Step 2 requires you to view the Info panel in this mode. Proceed directly to Step 3 if you are in Quick mode. The Levels dialog box opens and displays a histogram. This graph displays the distribution of the image's pixels at each of the 256 brightness levels. The histogram's highlights are on the right, mid-tones are in the center, and shadows are on the left.

Note: In addition to seeing the histogram of the composite RGB channel (the whole picture), you can also examine the histogram of only the Red, Green, or Blue channels by choosing one of them from the Channel drop-down box. Although you usually use the RGB channel to make changes to the whole picture, you may apply modifications to any one of the individual color channels of an image by choosing the channel from the Channel drop-down menu. You may also make changes to certain portions of your picture if you need to edit one but not all of it.

- To access the Info panel in Advanced mode, choose Window = Info.
- **To manually adjust the white point, use the eyedroppers in the Levels dialog box:**
  - ➢ After choosing the White Eyedropper tool, move the mouse over the picture.
  - ➢ Locate the lightest white point in the picture by examining the Info panel. To choose that spot, click on it. The lightest white has the highest RGB values.
- In Step 3, locate the deepest black region in the picture by using the Black Eyedropper tool once again. The deepest black has the lowest RGB values. When you set the pure black and pure white points, the remaining pixels are shifted between them. Altering the white and black triangles on the input sliders (just underneath the histogram) is another way to alter the white and black points. The Input Levels boxes may also be used to input values. The black, gray, and white triangles are each represented by one of the three boxes. Enter any number in the black and white boxes between 0 and 255.
- To remove color casts, use the Gray Eyedropper tool to find a neutral gray region of your picture where the Info panel displays equal values of red, green, and blue. A grayscale picture cannot be used with the Gray Eyedropper tool. You may choose a color channel using the Channel drop-down list. **You may also eliminate a color cast by executing one of the following if you're unsure where the neutral gray is:**
  - ➢ Select the Red channel and add cyan or red by dragging the midtone slider to the right or left, respectively.
  - ➢ Select the Green channel and add magenta or green by dragging the midtone slider to the right or left, respectively. To add yellow or blue, move the midtone slider to the right or left after selecting the Blue channel.
- You may use the Output Levels sliders at the bottom of the Levels dialog box if you need to reduce the contrast in your picture. The picture becomes brighter and the shadows less contrasty as the black triangle are moved to the right. The picture becomes darker and the highlights lose contrast as the white triangle is moved to the left.
- You may adjust the midtones, or gamma values, using the gray triangle input slider. The default value for gamma is 1.0. Drag the triangle to the left to lighten the midtones. Drag them to the right to make them darker. Another option is to provide a number.

+ Click OK to save your changes and exit the text box when you're finished.

If you don't want to manually alter your levels, you may choose the "Auto" option in the Levels text box. The Auto Levels command and Elements both make the same modifications. Clicking this button will cause the pixels to shift and the histogram to alter.

Modifying the Color

It may seem like your chances of receiving the color you choose are as slim as winning the state lottery. Sometimes a surprise color cast (a color shift) may be prevented at the filming stage. For instance, the camera's white balance may be adjusted for different lighting circumstances, or a flash or lens filter can be used—or not. Occasionally, one of the several adjustments in Elements might assist you in correcting the color after the fact. To create a distinctive impact, you may sometimes choose to alter the color of a picture. On the other hand, you may want to eliminate all of the colors in a picture to give it an antique appearance. Each of these color adjustments may be applied to a selection, a single layer, or the whole picture. You can rely on Elements to provide all of your color requirements. While Defringe Layers are only available in Advanced mode, all color adjustments may be applied in either Advanced or Quick mode.

Automatically eliminating color casts

If you've ever shot a photo at a school or workplace and it came out oddly green, it was most likely caused by the fluorescent lights above. To remove this green tint, use the Remove Color Cast command. This feature's objective is to remove the cast and alter the image's overall hue.
Simply follow these simple steps to improve your image:
+ In either Advanced or Quick mode, choose Enhance, then Adjust Color, and finally Remove Color Cast. The option to remove the color cast appears. To see your picture more clearly, move the dialog box.
+ To make a portion of your image white, black, or neutral gray, click on it. In our instance, I selected the white T-shirt worn by the girl in the picture on the left. The colors in the picture will alter to match if you choose a color. Which color is best? The answer will depend on the subject matter of your photograph. Feel free to experiment. Your

modification is now just a preview and won't become active until you click OK. The "Reset" button allows you to restore your picture to its original state after making changes.

- If you're not satisfied with your picture, repeat Step 2. Click OK to accept the change and exit the dialog box if you're OK with it.

If the Remove Color Cast command doesn't work, try adding a picture filter. For example, if there is too much green in your photo, use a magenta filter.

Modifying to Hue and Saturation

The Hue/Saturation command allows you to alter the hue, saturation, and luminance of the colors in a picture. The hue of your photograph is its color. The intensity or richness of a color is known as its saturation. The brightness level is also determined by lightness. **Use the Hue/Saturation command to change colors by doing the following:**

- In either Advanced or Quick mode, choose Enhance, then Adjust Color, and finally Adjust Hue/Saturation.
- The Hue/Saturation text box appears. Be careful to check the Preview box so you can see your changes. You may also use the Hue/Saturation command in Guided mode.
- Select Master from the Edit drop-down menu to change every color. Additionally, you may choose to change only one hue.
- **Drag the slider for any of the following properties to alter the colors as they appear:**
  - ➢ Hue: Drags all the colors in either a clockwise (drag right) or counterclockwise (drag left) direction around the color wheel.
  - ➢ **Saturation:** To make the colors richer or duller, drag to the right or left. By sliding the image to the left, you may make it seem grayscale.
  - ➢ **Lightness:** Adding white (drag right) raises the brightness levels, while adding black (drag left) lowers them.

The colors on the color wheel are shown in the order they appear in the top color bar at the bottom of the text box before you make any adjustments. The colors will appear in the bottom color bar when you make modifications. When you choose a particular color to modify, sliders appear between the color bars, allowing you to choose the color range. You may change the range of colors by clicking on the picture and using one of the Eyedropper tools. Additionally, the Hue/Saturation dialog box allows you to colorize photographs, which is helpful for creating sepia-colored images.

- (Optional) To convert the hues in your picture to a single color, choose Colorize. Use the Hue slider to adjust the color to the desired hue. The pure white and black pixels remain unchanged, while the intermediate gray pixels are colored.
- To save your changes and exit the text box, click OK. Use the Hue/Saturation command with the Colorize option to create tinted images similar to the one in the image below. You may also create choices in a grayscale picture and apply a different color to each pick. Using photos for this may be entertaining. Tinted photos may enhance even mediocre photos and give them a nostalgic or gloomy appearance.

Using Remove Color to get rid of color

All colors in an image, layer, or selection may be easily removed using the Remove Color command. To utilize this one-step operation, just choose Enhance, Adjust Color, and then Remove Color. Nevertheless, when you use this command to exclude colors, your picture may seem flat or lack contrast. To alter the contrast, Elements offers a variety of lighting tweaks. Auto Levels, Auto Contrast, and Levels are a few examples. You may convert a selection, a layer, or the whole picture to grayscale using the Convert to Black and White dialog box. Convert to Black and White after selecting Enhance. The Convert to Black and White command allows you to pick a conversion technique by first choosing an image style, in contrast to the Remove Color command, which removes color arbitrarily. You may further adjust the grayscale image's colors (red, green, or blue) or contrast with the Intensity sliders until it appears the way you want it to. **Footnote:** You are just altering the amount of information in the color channels; you are not adding color.

Using Replace Color to change colors

You may alter certain colors in a picture to other hues by using the Replace Color command. You start by making a mask of the colors you want to alter. A selection consisting of gray (partially chosen), black (unselected), and white (selected) regions is called a mask. The colors you choose may then have their hue and/or saturation changed.

The actions you must perform to alter the hue are as follows:

- In either Advanced or Quick mode, choose Enhance, then Adjust Color, and lastly Replace Color. The dialog window to change the color appears.
- **After checking the Preview box, choose either Selection or Image:**
  - ➢ The mask appears in the Preview section upon selection. Parts that have been partly chosen are gray, deselected parts are black, and selected areas are white.
  - ➢ Image displays the real picture in the Preview section.
- Use the Eyedropper tool to choose the colors you want in the Preview area or the picture.
- To add additional colors, use the Eyedropper tool's plus symbol (+) or click while holding down the shift key.
- Use the Eyedropper tool with the negative sign (–) or the Alt (or Option) key to remove a color.
- To fine-tune your choice, adjust the Fuzziness slider to the appropriate value. Colors that are comparable to the ones you chose may be added or removed from the selection based on the value. If the Fuzziness slider doesn't exactly provide the options you're looking for, you might try the Localized Color Clusters option. With this option,

you may choose several color clusters, or areas. If you want to pick more than one hue, it might assist you in making a clearer, more precise choice.

+ By manipulating the Hue and/or Saturation sliders, you may alter the color's hue or intensity. The Lightness slider allows you to adjust the image's brightness. Take caution not to push the Lightness slider too much while using it. If you drastically reduce the acoustic range, you risk making a mistake.
+ View the image window to see how it appears.
+ When you're finished, click OK to apply the changes and exit the dialog box.

Using Color Curves to Correct

Elements borrowed the widely used Curves tool from Photoshop. In contrast, Elements adds the descriptor "Color," although Color Curves isn't as sophisticated as its Photoshop counterpart. Nevertheless, in an attempt to enhance the variety of tones in color images, the Color Curves adjustment modifies the highlights, shadows, and midtones in each color channel. Consider using this command to pictures when backlighting makes the foreground components seem overly dark. In contrast, the correction is intended to correct images that seem overexposed and washed out. **This is a fantastic modification that can be applied to the whole picture, a layer, or a selection:**

+ Choose Enhance, then Adjust Color, and finally Adjust Color Curves after selecting a picture in either Advanced or Quick mode. The Adjust Color Curves dialog box appears.
+ To examine your picture in the after window and apply the alterations you want, choose a curve correction style from the choose a Style tab.

+ If you need to be more exact, use the sliders to change the brightness, contrast, and shadows. Then, move the sliders as needed. In the line in the lower right corner, the tones of your picture are dispersed. The range of tones in your picture is shown as a straight line when you initially view the Color Curves dialog box. The spectrum of tones

155

varies along with the straight line as you adjust the sliders. Remember that it's often simple to increase contrast in a picture by creating a little S-shaped curve. Equal portions of the highlights and shadows values should be reduced in order to accomplish this.

➢ To begin again, click the "Reset" button.

✦ Click OK after you've finished editing the picture.

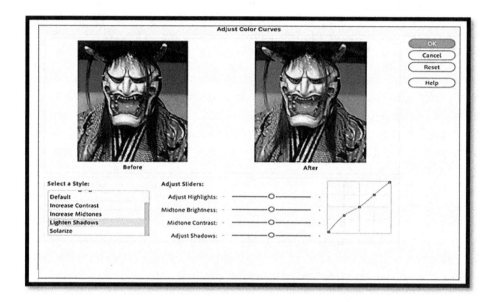

Modifying the tone of the skin

Occasionally, you can discover that the individuals in your photos have skin that is different from their own, such as red, green, or another hue. The "Adjust Color for Skin Tone" function in Elements may be used to correct that by altering the image's overall color and restoring the skin tones' natural hues.

How to utilize this is as follows:

- **Choose Advanced or Quick mode when opening your picture, then do one or both of the following steps:**
  - ➤ Select the layer that requires modification. If you have no layers, your whole picture is altered.
  - ➤ Select the areas of the skin that need adjustment. Only the regions you choose are changed. This is the best option if you are OK with the color of your other components and only want to alter the skin tones.
- Select Enhance > Adjust Color > Adjust Color for Skin Tone to change the color. The "Adjust Color for Skin Tone" dialog box appears. Guided mode also has this command.
- In the picture window, click on the area of the skin that need repair. Depending on your choices in Step 1, the command modifies the skin tone and the overall color of the picture, layer, or selection.
- **Click on a different location or experiment with the Skin and Ambient Light sliders if you're not satisfied with the outcome:**
  - ➤ Tan may alter the amount of brown in your skin.
  - ➤ You can use blush to alter the amount of red in your skin.
  - ➤ Temperature modifies the skin's general hue, making it either colder (left toward blue) or warmer (right toward red). To begin over, click the "Reset" button. To bail out, click Cancel, of course.
- Click OK to implement the adjustment and exit the text box if you're satisfied. It displays the newly toned skin.

Layers defringing

Fringed selections are a dead giveaway for hurriedly assembled images. Not the adorable sort that dangles from your sofa or leather jacket. The unsightly kind, that is, composed of background pixels that surround the boundaries of your selections.

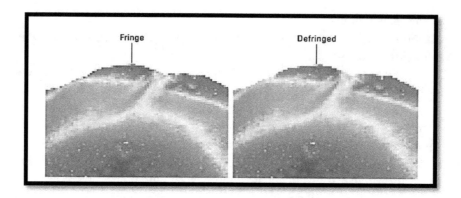

A selection will always be moved or copied with some background pixels when you move or paste it. These pixels are known as fringes or rims. Thankfully, the Defringe command replaces the colors of the pixels on the borders with the colors of neighboring pixels that lack the background color. In this instance, I placed the red blossom on a white backdrop after removing it from a blue one. Some of the backdrop pixels that appear as a blue border are part of our choices. The blue pixels on the edge are changed to the color of nearby pixels, such as red, via the Defringe order.

Do the following if you want to violate your choice:

+ Drag and drop a selection into a new document in Advanced or Quick mode, or copy and paste a selection onto an existing or new layer.
+ Select Enhance, followed by Adjust Color and Defringe Layer.
+ The dialog window for Defringe appears.
+ The amount of pixels you want to alter might be entered. To see whether it works, you might enter 1 or 2 first. You may need to provide a little higher number if not.
+ Click OK to close the box and accept the amount.

Getting rid of haze

You may rapidly remove haze from your images with the help of elements' practical and straightforward function. Haze might worsen depending on the weather and time of day. When light strikes dust, dirt, and other airborne particles, haze is created. Increasing the contrast and sharpness of your photograph may sometimes assist reduce the hazy effect. But it's simpler than ever to get rid of it using this program. **Use these steps to get rid of haze in your pictures:**

+ Use either Quick or Advanced mode to open a picture.
+ Then choose "Enhance" and "Haze Removal." The text box for Haze Removal appears.
+ By sliding the slider, you may choose your Haze Reduction option. There will be less haze as you glide to the right.
+ Move the slider to adjust the sensitivity level. The quantity of haze observed will grow as you move the slider to the right.
+ To see the outcomes, toggle the "Before and After" option, then click "OK."

Using picture filters to change the color temperature

The color temperature of each form of light varies. A blue picture is one that was captured in light with a higher color temperature. In contrast, a picture shot at a lower color temperature is yellow. Photographers used to place tinted glass screens in front of their lenses to alter the light's color temperature. They used this to add a little color for cool effects or to warm up or chill down pictures. You may create these effects on your computer by using Elements' Photo Filter command. **To utilize the Photo Filter setting, follow these steps:**

- Select Filter > Adjustments > Photo Filter in either Advanced or Quick mode. The window box for the Photo Filter appears. By creating a photo-filter adjustment layer, you may also apply the picture filter to a single layer.
- Choose Filter from the drop-down option in the text field to choose a pre-set filter. Choose Color from the Color Picker to choose the color of your filter. **A brief description of each of the preset filters is provided below:**
  - ➤ **Warming Filter (85), (81), and (LBA):** These modify an image's white balance to make the colors more yellow or warmer. Similar to (85) and (LBA), filter (81) works best for little modifications.
  - ➤ **Cooling Filter (80), (82), and (LBB):** These likewise modify the displayed white balance, but they make the colors bluer or cooler rather than warmer. Filter (82) is similar to (80) and (LBB), however it may be adjusted somewhat.
  - ➤ **Red, Orange, Yellow, and so forth:** A photo's hue, or color, may be altered using the different color filters. To add a particular effect or attempt to remove a color cast, use a color filter.
- The Density slider allows you to customize how much color is added to your picture.
- Select the Preserve Luminosity option to prevent your picture from being darkened by the photo filter.
- Click OK to apply your filter and exit the box. Before you snap the photo, make sure the white balance on your camera is adjusted for the ambient illumination. You'll be able to change colors less often as a result.

Constructing a color map

The "color mappers" commands in Elements allow you to alter an image's colors by allocating them to various values. The Filter → Adjustments menu contains the color mappers. **Each command is demonstrated in the image below, and they are all explained in the list below:**

- **Equalize:** This mapper first determines which pixels are the brightest and darkest, then assigns them black and white values to equalize the picture. The remaining pixels are then moved about among the grayscale values. The precise outcome relies on how you present yourself.
- **Gradient Map:** This command links the colors of a gradient of your choice to the tonal range of a picture. For instance, the shadow, highlight, and midtone sections are mapped to orange, green, and purple.
- **Invert:** This sentence creates a kind of negative by flipping all of the colors in your picture. Colors shift into their complementary hues, and black becomes white. White, gray, or black are the outcomes of properly combining complimentary hues, which are opposite each other on the color wheel. Thus, red becomes cyan, blue becomes yellow, and so on.
- **Posterize:** This command reduces the amount of brightness levels in your picture. Select a level number from 2 to 255. Higher values give the picture a more photographic appearance, while lower values give it the appearance of an artwork or poster.
- **Threshold:** All pixels in your picture that are darker than a certain value are converted black, and all pixels that are brighter than that value are turned white when the threshold is set. To get a variety of high contrast effects, you may adjust the threshold amount.

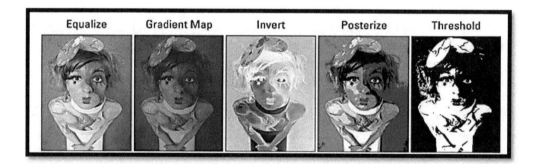

Modifying Clarity

Once a picture has the proper color and contrast and any defects have been corrected, you may concentrate on making it more readable. You may have used the healing tools to correct minor imperfections, but you may need to employ a filter if your picture has more serious issues, such as dust, scratches, or artifacts (such as blocky pixels or halos). After your picture has been cleaned sufficiently, the last step is to sharpen it. Why hold off till the end? It is sometimes possible to reduce the clarity and sharpness of a picture while enhancing the color and contrast and eliminating imperfections. Therefore, before you begin sharpening the picture, make sure it is as soft as possible. After sharpening a significant portion of your picture, you may need to make further lighting changes since sharpening intensifies contrast. Lastly, after all this discussion about sharpening, I realize this may seem odd, but occasionally you also need to blur your picture. Blurring may smooth distracting backgrounds to make the primary topic stand out more, remove unpleasant patterns that appear during scanning, or even give the picture a moving appearance.

Eliminating dust, scratches, noise, and artifacts

Surprisingly, the tools you need to clean up your photographs may be found under the Filter > Noise submenu in either Advanced or Quick mode. The Add Noise filter is the only one that is unable to conceal dust, noise, scratches, and imperfections. **Junk may be eliminated by doing the following:**

+ **Despeckle:** Reduces contrast without altering the image's borders, making the dust in your picture less noticeable. You could notice that your picture is a bit hazy since the garbage is being disguised. I hope the margins remain distinct.

+ **Dust & Scratches:** To conceal the dust and scratches in your photograph, blur the undesirable areas. It searches for sudden shifts in tone. Select the desired Radius number, which indicates the size of the blurred region. The threshold number, which instructs the software on how much contrast between pixels it must detect before blurring them, may also be changed. Because it might remove features and exacerbate an already poor picture, use this filter cautiously.

+ **Median:** Reduces contrast around areas of dust. In summary, the bright areas get darker and the dark spots lighter as a result of the filter's many intricate functions. The remainder of the picture remains unchanged. The size of the area that will be altered is determined by the radius you choose.

+ **Reduce Noise:** This function is designed to eliminate luminance noise and other extraneous elements from your picture. Luminance noise is a kind of grayscale noise that makes images seem excessively gritty. Make the following choices to reduce the noise in your image:
  ➢ **Strength:** Select the desired level of noise suppression.
  ➢ Preserve features: A larger percentage reduces the amount of noise removed while protecting edges and features.
  ➢ Eliminate arbitrary colored pixels to reduce color noise.
  ➢ **Eliminate JPEG Artifact:** Get rid of the blocks and halos that may show up when JPEG compression is done poorly.

Blurring when necessary

It may seem odd that someone would wish to blur a picture. To correct issues like excessive graininess or an unsatisfactory moiré pattern, you may need to blur the picture. To remove distracting components or to make the foreground objects more prominent and the primary focus, you may often even wish to blur the backdrop of a photograph. The Filter > Blur menu contains all of the blurring instructions in Advanced or Quick mode. **Conversely, the Tools panel has the Blur tool:**

- **Average:** This one-step filter determines the picture or selection's average value and applies that value to the region. It may be used to smooth out portions of your picture that are too noisy.
- **Blur:** This one-step filter also blurs the whole picture by a predetermined amount.
- **Blur More:** This one-step blur filter accomplishes the same goal as Blur but amplifies the impact.
- **Gaussian Blur:** You'll probably use this blur filter the most. You may change the blurry quality by adjusting the Radius parameter.

The Gaussian Blur filter may be used to conceal moiré patterns in scanned images. Halftone images produce a moiré pattern when scanned. A digital picture with continuous tones, such as a photograph, is converted into a repeating line pattern on the screen (often 85 to 150 lines per inch). A halftone is then created by printing this design. When you scan that halftone, a second design is created and superimposed on top of the original pattern. When these two distinct designs collide, a terrible moiré pattern is created. The only thing the Gaussian Blur filter does is mix the dots and blur the pattern; it doesn't remove the moiré. Find a suitable balance between less moiré and less focus by using the Radius tool. If your scanning program offers a descreen filter, you may use it to try to remove the moiré pattern from scanned halftones. **When scanning the halftone picture, you may also utilize it.**

- **Lens Blur:** Refer to the text that follows this list for further details on the purpose and use of this blur filter.
- **Motion Blur:** This filter gives the impression that moving things have blurred the borders of pictures. The blur's distance and motion angle are up to you. Make sure to choose the Preview option so you can see the outcome as you enter your numbers.
- **Radial Blur:** Do you want to give the impression that a Ferris wheel or other circular object is in motion? This filter creates a circular blur effect. Decide on the desired amount of blur. The blur will follow the thumbnail's circular lines if you choose the Spin technique. Another option is Zoom, which gives the impression that you are zooming in by blurring your picture along radial lines. Decide on the desired quality level. Elements allows you to choose between Draft (quick but fuzzy), Good, and Best (slow but smooth) due to the slowness of the Radial Blur filter. It is only via large, high-quality photos that one can distinguish between Good and Best. Lastly, slide the blur photo thumbnail to the desired location for the blur's center.
- **Smart Blur:** You may choose how the blur is applied with this filter. Decide on the desired settings for the cutoff and radius. Make adjustments after setting the initial figure for both to a lower value. **Select the desired quality option from the drop-down menu. Select a mode:**
  - Normal blurs the whole selection or picture.
  - Edge just employs black and white in the blurred pixels and only blurs the borders of your items.

➢ Overlay Edge blurs just the edges as well, but it only adds white to the pixels that are blurred.

ᛋ The Surface Blur filter blurs the image's center or surface rather than its borders. If you want to blur everything else while maintaining the details on the edges, use this filter.

You can adjust how deep or narrow the depth of field is if you have ever experimented with the aperture settings on your camera. The region of an image that remains in focus, whether it is in front of or behind the focal point, is known as the plane of focus. The depth of field indicates the relative emphasis of the foreground and background parts. The Lens Blur filter may be used to enhance an image's depth of field after it has been shot. This enables you to selectively concentrate on certain areas of a fully focused image.

Here's how you use the Lens Blur filter:

ᛋ Choose Lens Blur under Filter >Blur. The Lens Blur Filter text box appears.

ᛋ Select the Preview mode. With the More Accurate option, a brief preview of the finished picture is seen, but not with the quicker alternative.

ᛋ Select your Source from the drop-down option if you have one for your depth map. A transparency or a layer mask is your options. The filter uses a depth map to determine the blur. By creating a layer mask on your image layer and filling it with a white-to-black gradient, you can get this shallow depth-of-field effect. Where you want the greatest blur or the least focus, fill it with white; where you want the most focus, fill it with black. By selecting Transparency, you may blur a picture and increase its transparency.

ᛋ By using the Blur Focal Distance slider, you may adjust how crisp or fuzzy a certain portion of the picture appears. Another option is to click the crosshair on the region of the picture that requires complete focus. You may move the slider to choose a number. Another way to flip the depth map source is to choose "Invert."

ᛋ Select an Iris shape, such as an octagon or triangle, from the Shape drop-down option. You may make it resemble the opening blades on a camera lens by adjusting the Iris settings. You must describe the form of the lens, its rotation, blade curvature (the smoothness of the iris's sides), and radius (the size of the iris).

+ For Specular Highlights, adjust the area's brightness and threshold. The brightest areas of a picture are averaged by the Lens Blur filter. Some of the brightest areas may seem gray if this isn't fixed. The highlights that should seem very white are called specular highlights. They may be maintained using the Specular Highlights settings. By adjusting the threshold number, you may choose which highlights should be specular (remain white). Establish a Brightness amount to determine how bright to make any hazy spots clear once more.

+ Move the Amount slider in the Noise section to restore noise in your picture. To add noise that doesn't alter the color, choose monochromatic. Any noise or film grain in a picture is eliminated when it is blurred. This absence of noise might give the picture a wobbly or unnatural appearance to many individuals.

+ Click OK to apply the Lens Blur and exit the text box.

Sharpening to increase concentration

Of course, if your photos don't need any color, contrast, or defect repair, you may go ahead and sharpen them immediately. Sometimes digital camera or scanner images are a little soft, and this isn't because the tones have been altered. Sometimes you may wish to sharpen a certain section of your picture to make it stand out more. Once a picture has been captured, it cannot be made clearer. You may, however, fake it rather well. The way all sharpening tools function is by increasing the visibility of cell differences. The stronger contrast helps the sharper lines seem better, giving the impression that the focus is better. Remember that minor sections may also be sharpened using the Sharpen tool. **The two sharpening orders signify the following:**

+ The best sharpening tool is the Unsharp Mask. Both Advanced and Quick modes are available in the Enhance menu. The darkroom technique is where the term "Unsharp Mask" originates. You may adjust the amount to be sharpened and the width of the areas to be sharpened using a number of parameters. **To get the precise level of sharpness you want, use them:**

  ➢ **Quantity:** Select between 1% and 500% edge sharpening. As the number increases, the contrast between the pixels at the margins increases. Start with a value of no more than 100%. Usually, this allows for a nice contrast without seeming too gritty.

  ➢ The radius, which may range from 0.1 to 250 pixels, is the width of the edges that the filter will enhance. The greater the value, the greater the advantage. The value you choose is heavily influenced by the image's resolution. For low-resolution picture files, a lower radius number is required. For high-resolution images, a higher value is required. To assist you determine a starting radius value, divide the resolution of your picture by 150. If you choose a number that is too high, the borders of your image will seem overly "contrasty" or even "goopy." If you have a 300 ppi picture, set the radius to 2, for example, and then adjust it with your eye.

  ➢ **Threshold:** Determine how much brightness difference (between 0 and 255) must exist between adjacent pixels before the edge is sharpened. There is no difference in contrast, but edges are sharper when the value is lower. Higher values only make things crisper when two photos close to one other have drastically contrasting contrasts. Unless your picture is really grainy, you should leave the threshold at 0. When the number is set too high, the transitions between sharpened and unsharpened regions may seem odd. The numbers you provide for Amount and Radius may sometimes sharpen the image nicely, but they can also introduce excessive noise, or grain, into the picture. Sometimes this noise may be reduced by raising the threshold number.

✦ **Adjust Sharpness:** One option for adjusting the sharpness of your photos is Unsharp Mask. The Adjust Sharpness command is the other one. This option allows you to adjust the amount of sharpness that is applied to regions that are highlighted and shadowed. Additionally, you have a range of sharpening techniques to choose from. **The many options available to you are as follows:**

➢ Radius and Amount function similarly to the Unsharp Mask command.

➢ **Preset:** You may save your picture editing methods as a preset, which you can load and use at a later time.

➢ **Remove:** Select your algorithm for sharpening. Gaussian Blur is activated when the Unsharp Mask command is used. Lens Blur searches for features in a picture and attempts to preserve them while eliminating the unsightly halos that may appear during sharpening. Motion Blur attempts to eliminate the blur that occurs when the subject moves or when the camera is moved.

➢ **Angle:** Indicate the direction of motion to the Motion Blur algorithm, which was covered in the previous paragraph.

➢ **Shadows/Highlights:** The Highlights and Shadows sections allow you to adjust how crisp your picture is. To choose the desired level of sharpness, use the Fade Amount parameter. The Tonal Width option allows you to choose the range of tones you want to sharpen. You can only enhance the highlights and shadows by moving the slider to the right. Lastly, you may choose the Radius parameter to determine how much space is utilized to determine if a pixel is in the highlight or shadow region. Move the slider to the right to choose a larger region.

Opening the eyelids that were closed

The individuals in your photo don't always stare straight ahead and grin at the same time. With this tool, you can at least address the eye issue. Using the Open Closed Eyes tool, you may combine two photos of the same person or people with their eyes open to create a charming hero shot.

What you do is this:

- Use either Quick or Advanced mode to open a picture. You may open a photo from the Organizer, the Photo Bin, or your PC.
- After selecting Enhance, choose Open Closed Eyes. Additionally, you may choose the Open Closed Eyes button from the tool's settings after selecting the Eye tool in the Tools panel. The dialog window for Open Closed Eyes appears. The region of the dialog box that will be impacted by the modifications is shown by a circle.
- Select a picture to serve as your eye source.
- To apply the source picture, click on it. It automatically substitutes the closed eyes with the eyes from the original picture.

Adding color to a picture

This improvement allows you to add color to black-and-white photographs or change the color of colorful pictures. Indeed, there are a few methods to colorize images in Elements, such using the Brush tool in Color Blend mode or Hue/Saturation, but this approach will make your image seem more aged and hand-painted. **To add color to a photograph, follow these steps:**

- Use either Quick or Advanced mode to open a picture.
- Click on "Enhance" and then "Colorize Photo." Note that the first time you use this option; you may be prompted to download a file. The Colorize Photo text box appears.
- Both Auto and Manual modes are available.
- If you choose Auto mode, you may pick from four pre-sets in Basic mode. Each one adds contrast to the picture.
- **To make more modifications, choose "Manual" mode and follow these steps:**
  - Use the Lasso tool or Quick Selection to choose an area that needs extra color. The Quick Selection tool has a Size slider that allows you to adjust the tool's width.
  - Use the Add to or Subtract from buttons on each tool to further shape the region of your choice. Additionally, you may add by using the Shift key and remove by pressing the Option/Alt key.
  - Choose the Droplet Tool and click within the area you want to colorize when you're ready.
  - Select the color swatch you want to use from the Color Palette or the All Applicable Colors screen. Turn off the Show Droplets option at the bottom to get rid of the Droplet icons from your picture.
  - If you would like, repeat the instructions. If you're not familiar with the Manual approach, click the arrow to the right of the term "Manual". You may watch a brief video on Adobe.com that demonstrates how to colorize photos.
- Click OK if you're happy with what you see. To begin over, click the "Reset" button.

Skin smoothing

Making individuals seem better online than they do in person is another thing that Elements enables you to achieve. Fortunately, the new Smooth Skin function prevents you from going mad and erasing any evidence of your existence. Rather, it only helps people seem younger by reducing wrinkles and creases.

To get smooth skin, do the following:
- Use either Quick or Advanced mode to open a picture.
- Select Smooth Skin after selecting Enhance. The Smooth Skin text box appears. The region of the dialog box that will be impacted by the changes is shown by a circle.
- To apply the required level of smoothing, use the Smoothness slider.
- Flip your "Before and After" button to view the results.
- If you are satisfied with the outcome, click OK. If not, you may click Reset or Cancel.

If you feel that your subject needs a little more "work," you may utilize the "Perfect Portrait" tool in Guided Edit mode, which contains the Smooth Skin feature and tools to enhance eyes, darken eyebrows, whiten teeth, and make other adjustments.

Modifying facial characteristics

The Adjust Facial Features command is a simplified, automated version of the popular Liquify function. Many magazine photos may be fixed with this effective technique. Although you can't manually alter many aspects using Adjust Facial Features, the outcome is rather potent and the interface is easy to use. Prepare yourself for requests to alter photos from friends and family!

How to utilize this is as follows:
- Use either Quick or Advanced mode to open a picture.
- Then choose "Enhance" and "Adjust Facial Features." The "Adjust Facial Features" dialog box appears. The section of the dialog box that will be altered by the modifications is surrounded by a circle. Remember those first tests to determine if it's a face. I tried with a picture of a cat. Not a chance.
- The sliders allow you to adjust your face, including your eyes, nose, lips, chin, and face.
- The Face Tilt tool allows you to adjust the face's various angles.
- Flip your "Before and After" button to view the results.
- Are you feeling well? Click "OK." Disappointed? Select "Reset" to begin again.

Choose Preferences > Performance and make sure the Use Graphic Processor option is selected to guarantee quicker and better performance when using tools like Adjust Facial tools and the Lens Blur and Liquify filters.

Overlays That Move

Moving Overlays is an entertaining animation application that allows you to add moving information from three distinct categories to your still photographs.

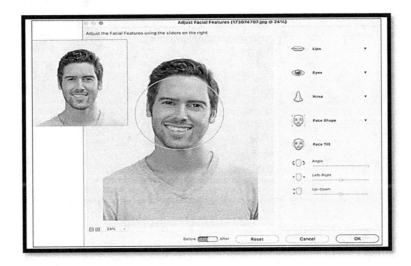

Follow these steps to build moving layers:

- Use either Quick or Advanced mode to open a picture.
- After selecting Enhance, choose Moving Overlays. The text box for Moving Overlays appears.
- From the drop-down option on the right side of the text box, choose Frames, Overlays, or Graphics.
- Double-click the motion overlay you want to apply to the picture. Remember that you may drag a handle in the accompanying transform box to adjust the size of a frame or picture. Making a preview takes Elements a minute or two.
- By selecting the "Protect Subject" option, you may decide to hide your motion material behind your still picture. You may also utilize the Opacity slider to reduce the opaqueness of your motion content.
- The Refine Overlay button may be used to eliminate information. The sliders allow you to adjust your brush's size and opacity. If you change your mind, you can always add it back in using the "Add" button.
- Under your picture, click the Play/Stop button. The motion effect has been applied to your photo, as you can see in the picture below.
- When you are satisfied with the outcome, click the "Export" button at the bottom of the box.

169

Your file may be exported as an MP4 movie or an animated GIF. Following that, you may utilize the file on your iPhone, Facebook, Twitter, and websites.

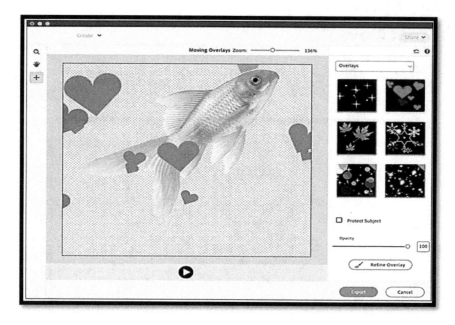

Moving Pictures

With the Moving Photos tool, you can give your still photos a little movement. You'll be amazed at how simple it is, and you'll question how Adobe's programmers managed to conceal all the intricate technical details behind the scenes.

Instructions for using it:

- Use either Quick or Advanced mode to open a picture.
- Next, choose "Enhance" and "Moving Photos." The straightforward Moving Photos box appears.
- Double-click the motion effect on the right side of the dialog box that you want to apply to your picture. Give Elements a few moments to create a preview.
- Under your picture, click the Play/Stop button. The motion effect is applied to your photo, which is amazing.
- Because the 3D Effect is used by default, the picture has additional depth. Turn it off to see it without the 3D effect.
- Click the Export button at the bottom of the dialog box if you're satisfied with the file.

You may turn your moving picture into an animated GIF or MP4 file. Show it out by posting or tweeting about it on social media.

Elements That Move

Another tool for enhancing animated photos is provided by Elements. You may make some portions of a static picture move by using the Moving Elements function.

It's simple and a lot of fun. How to use it:

- Use either Quick or Advanced mode to open a picture.
- Simply choose "Enhance" and then "Moving Elements." The text box for Moving Elements appears.

- On the right side of the dialog box, choose the area you want to add motion to. For our picture, I chose the sky. Please note that for this feature, it may be better to make a rough selection rather than a very accurate one. If you select "Manual," you can use the Brush tool, the Quick Select tool, or the Magic Wand (Auto) for the selection. If you select the Show Mask option, a red overlay will appear over your selection.
- Drag the motion in the direction you want by using the arrow button. A turquoise direction arrow is seen in the figure below. For optimal effects, use fewer arrows rather than more.
- Set the desired pace for the selection using the speed slider, and then click "Select All" to move the whole selection at that speed.
- Click the Play button, which resembles a white arrow on a black circle, to watch a preview of your picture. When you're finished, click the Export button, and then click "Done" to dismiss the box. Your moving picture will be converted into an MP4 file.

Making Sensible Use of the Smart Brush Tools

You can use the Smart Brush and Detail Smart Brush tools to selectively apply a special effect or image adjustment to all or a portion of your image, and even better, these adjustments and effects are applied through an adjustment layer, which means they remain on top of your layers and do not permanently alter the pixels in your image. You can also edit or remove changes as needed. **To use the Smart Brush tool, follow these steps:**

- In Advanced mode, choose the Smart Brush tool from the toolbar. If the Detail Smart Brush tool is shown, you may also hit F or Shift+F. The tool symbol resembles a paintbrush for painting a home.
- From the Tool Options' Preset Picker drop-down list, choose your specific preset adjustment after selecting an adjustment category. The Preset menu contains adjustments ranging from Photographic effects (such as an old Yellowed Photo) to Nature effects (such as Create a Sunset, which gives your image a warm, orange glow). The Textures category contains thirteen presets, some of which are Broken Glass and Old Paper. Use these textures with your smart brushes to add interest to backgrounds and other image elements, such as adding a Brick wall texture to that white wall in your shot if it's not very interesting, or adding a satin ripple to the drop cloth you placed behind your photo to break up the background if it looks a little boring.
- Select the desired brush parameters, such as size, and adjust hardness, spacing, roundness, and angle using the Brush Settings drop-down panel.
- Paint an adjustment on the layer of your picture that you want to modify. When you make your initial paint stroke, a new adjustment layer is created instantly, along with the accompanying layer mask. The Smart Brush tool looks for borders in your picture and snaps to them. A selection border also appears while you brush.

- Using the Add and Subtract Smart Brush modes in the Tool Options, you may add to and subtract from your altered area to fine-tune it. When you add anything to your adjusted area, it becomes whiter; when you take something away from your adjusted area, it becomes blacker. In other words, you are altering your layer mask.
- **Make the necessary adjustments in the text box:**
  - To refine the region you have chosen, pick "Refine Edge" from the Tool Options menu.
  - To apply the change to the area that is not chosen, pick "Inverse" from the Tool Options.
  - Double-clicking the Adjustment Layer pin on your image will reveal a small, square, black-and-red gear icon. Double-clicking the pin will bring up the text box for the adjustment you wish to make. Double-clicking the Shoebox photo change (under Photographic) is one way to open the Hue/Saturation dialog box. Additionally, you may right-click and choose "Change Level Settings." You can also select "Delete Adjustment" and "Hide Selection" with the same option.
- Click OK.
- To deselect your selection when you're finished, just pick pick > Deselect.

Additional Smart Brush changes may be made by restarting the Smart Brush tool after finishing an effect. **To utilize the Detail Smart Brush tool, follow these steps:**
- In Advanced mode, choose the Detail Smart Brush tool from the toolbar. The tool icon is a pen, and if you can see the Smart Brush tool, you can also hit F or Shift+F. The flyout menu for this tool and the Smart Brush tool is the same.
- From the Preset Picker drop-down list in the Tool Options, choose the desired adjustment category and then the desired preset adjustment.
- Select your preferred brush size and tip from the Brush Preset Picker drop-down list. To get the desired effect, you may adjust the brush's tip and size, and you can also choose

from various brush preset libraries using the Brush drop-down menu in the Brush tip preset menu.

⊥ Paint an adjustment on the section of your picture that you want. An adjustment layer and a layer mask are created automatically when you apply your initial paint stroke.

⊥ Use the Smart Brush tool by following Steps 5 through 8 in the previous list.

CHAPTER FOURTEEN
EVERYTHING ABOUT SELECTIONS

Specifying Selections

When you specify a selection, you indicate the area of a picture that you want to work with. It is believed that every item in a selection was picked. Nothing that isn't on the list gets picked. Only the selected portion may be altered after a selection. The portion that was not selected remains unchanged. The region you choose may easily be copied and pasted into another picture. The dotted line that appears around the region you pick while making a selection is known as a selection border, outline, or marquee. Elements is a high-tech image tool that also allows you to choose just certain pixels, allowing you to generate soft-edged selections. A selection with soft edges may be created by feathering it or by using a mask. Before uploading the picture, make sure your photo editor is in Advanced mode rather than Quick, Guided, or the Organizer for all of these selection techniques to function.

Making Elliptical and Rectangular Selections

If you know how to drag a mouse, you can learn how to utilize the Rectangular and Elliptical Marquee tools. If you want a rectangular or elliptical form, use one of these selecting tools as they are the simplest to use. The rectangle Marquee tool allows you to produce rectangle choices, even square ones, as the name implies. This tool works well for highlighting the key elements of a photo and eliminating unnecessary background. **The following choices may be made using this tool:**

- The Tools panel has the Rectangular Marquee tool. Choose it. The instrument has a square-like appearance with dots on it. You may also hit M to access the tool. If the tool is not visible, press M once again.
- From one corner to the other, you may drag the region you want to pick. As you drag, the selection boundary appears. The menu moves in tandem with your mouse movements.
- The mouse button should be released. Your rectangle selection is now complete.

The Elliptical Marquee tool is designed for elliptical or circular selections. This tool makes it simple to choose clocks, balloons, and other circular objects.

The Elliptical Marquee may be used as follows:

- The Tools panel has the Elliptical Marquee tool. Choose it. The instrument has a circle-like appearance with dots on it. Additionally, you may hit M to access this tool if it is displayed. Press M once more if it isn't. If using the keyboard shortcut does not cycle between the tools, choose Preferences > General and deselect Use Shift Key for Tool Switch.
- To choose a portion of the picture, place the crosshair near to it and move it around. This tool allows you to drag from one location on the ellipse to another. As you drag, the selection boundary appears.
- When you're satisfied with the choice, let go of the mouse button. An elliptical option is now available to you. You may drag within the selection border to relocate it if your pick isn't exactly in the center of the element.

You may move the selection as you create it by holding down the spacebar and dragging with either of the Marquee tools.

Using Shift and Alt to perfect squares and circles (Mac option)

Sometimes you have to choose something that is precisely round or square. Simply begin moving and use the Shift key to do this. Once you've chosen, let go of the mouse button and press the Shift key. You may also adjust the number to 1:1 in the Tool Options. Making an elliptical selection from the center outward is often simple. Press the mouse button where you want the center to be before you begin sketching. Next, drag after pressing Alt (or Option on a Mac). Once you have made your choice, let go of the mouse button and press the Alt (or Option on a Mac) key. If you wish to draw a square or circle from the center straight out, use the Shift key as well. Once you have made your choice, let go of the Shift+Alt (or Shift+Option on a Mac) keys.

Using the Marquee selections

The Marquee tools provide you with additional choices when you need to make precise selections at certain sizes. Soft-edged decisions may also be made. Just keep in mind that before using the Marquee tools to choose, you must first pick the settings under the Tool settings. Options cannot be utilized again after a choice has been made. Another option is to feather a selection after the fact by selecting and then feathering.

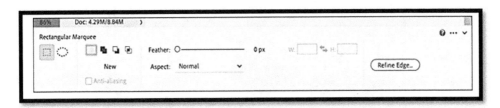

The many marquee options available to you are as follows:

- Feather: This gives your choice a softer edge. The slider allows you to adjust the image's softness by setting a value between 0 and 250 pixels. As the value increases, the edges get softer. Very little feathering may be used to blend a piece into an existing backdrop or to create gentle transitions between selected collage components. Larger quantities are often used when combining several layers such that one picture fades into another. Simply choose an element and hit "Inverse." This will remove the backdrop if you simply want the piece's soft border. Remember that pixels with the soft edges were only partially picked.
- **Anti-aliasing:** This function lessens the visibility of sharp edges by somewhat smoothing down the edges of an elliptical or other oddly shaped selection. The width of a smooth edge is always one pixel. I advise you to leave this option selected for your options. This might assist you in creating seamless transitions between various options while creating collages.
- **Aspect:** The Aspect drop-down menu has three choices:
  - ➢ **Normal:** You may drag a selection of any size in this default mode.
  - ➢ **Set Ratio:** Allow you to choose a set width to height ratio. For instance, regardless of size, if you input 3 for width and 1 for height, you will always receive a selection that is three times as large as it is high.
  - ➢ **Fixed Size:** This option allows you to choose the desired height and width. This setting might be useful when selecting many options that need to have the same size.
- **Height (H) and Width (W):** These two boxes are named Height (H) and Width (W). You must also enter the desired numbers in the fields if you choose Fixed Ratio or Fixed Size from the Aspect drop-down menu. Click the arrow button with two heads between the width and height values to adjust them.

The Width and Height text boxes feature pixels (px) as the unit of measurement, although you are not required to use them. Pixels, inches (in), centimeters (cm), millimeters (mm), points (pt), picas (pc), and percentages (%) are all examples of numbers that Elements can comprehend. After entering your number, input the term or abbreviation for the unit you're using.

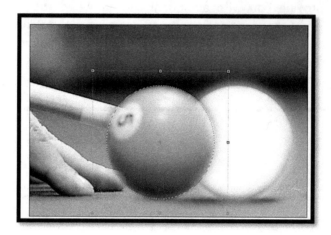

Using the Lasso Tools to Make Freeform Selections

Rectangles and ellipses cannot be utilized for selection. Life isn't like that at all. Many inanimate items and the majority of moving objects exhibit some kind of undulation. Fortunately, Elements provided us with the Lasso tools since it understood that these shapes would need to be collected. You may create any kind of freehand selection you can imagine with the Lasso tools. **Elements offers three different kinds of Lasso tools for free:**

- Lasso
- Polygonal
- Magnetic

Though they do it in somewhat different ways, all three tools are designed to create freeform decisions. A steady hand is all you need to utilize these tools. As you utilize the Lasso tools more, your drawing skills will improve. Don't stress if your initial choice of lasso isn't flawless. You have the option to add to or remove your selection at any moment. If you discover that you really like the Lasso tools, you may want to get a digital drawing pad and pen. This program makes it easy to trace, draw, and paint on the computer. After seeing what this accomplishes, many users vow they will never use a mouse again. Those that utilize laptops will find this extremely useful. Attempting to sketch accurately on a trackpad may be really annoying.

Using the Lasso tool to select

In digital form, using the Lasso tool is similar to drawing a line around an item on paper. That's easy. Additionally, the Tool Options only have three choices: **Refine Edge, Feather, and Anti-aliasing. Here's how to utilize the Lasso selection tool:**

+ **The Tools panel has the Lasso tool. Choose it:** It is the instrument that resembles a rope. The L key is another option. To navigate between the many Lasso flavors if the Lasso tool is not visible, press L. Remember that the Tool menu underneath the picture is another way to access any of the Lasso tools.

+ **Move the cursor anywhere along the edge of an item to choose it:** The leading point of the cursor is the protruding end of the rope. If you need a better view of an object's edge, you may use the Zoom tool or, for a quicker view, use Control++ (CMD++ on a Mac). In this image, I started at the top of the sunflower.

+ **Trace around the item of your choice while holding down the mouse button:** Try to limit your choices to the things you want. As you sketch around the item, an outline travels with the mouse pointer. Make an effort to hold onto the mouse button until you return to your starting position. Elements assumes that you are finished when you release the mouse button, and it returns the selection to the beginning point. A straight line is drawn across your picture by Elements if you release the button too quickly.

+ **Continue tracing around the item before returning to your starting point. To end the selection, release the mouse button:** A selection boundary that corresponds to your lasso line appears. When you return to your starting point, look for a little circle that appears adjacent to your lasso cursor. You can see if you're concluding the selection correctly by looking at this symbol.

Using the Polygonal Lasso tool straight

The Polygonal Lasso tool is designed to choose any object with straight edges. Pyramids, staircases, skyscrapers, barns, and so forth come to mind. Additionally, it functions somewhat differently from the Lasso tool. The Polygonal Lasso cannot be used to move the portion around. Instead, you click at the edges of the piece you want to select and release the mouse button. The Polygonal Lasso tool may be stretched and twisted like a rubber band.

Lasso Cursor

To choose using the Polygonal Lasso tool, follow these steps:

+ The Tools panel has the Polygonal Lasso tool. Choose it. The L key may also be used to switch between the various Lasso tools. The instrument resembles a straight-sided lasso rope.

+ Click and let go at any point to begin the Polygonal Lasso selection line. I start in a corner most of the time.

+ Click at the next corner of the item after moving the mouse (do not drag). Click again and go to every area of your element. As you click on various spots, see how the line lengthens.

+ Click to dismiss the option and go back to where you were before. Look for a little circle that appears next to your lasso cursor when you return to the beginning place. You are closing the selection correctly if you see this circle.

Footnote: Elements allows you to double-click at any point, which returns the selection to the beginning. Once the polygonal lasso line is closed, a selection boundary appears.

Using the Magnetic Lasso tool to snap

The third Lasso on the squad is the Magnetic Lasso. I dislike this Lasso tool since it might be difficult to use. However, I will demonstrate its operation so that you may decide whether or not to utilize it. The Magnetic Lasso tool may be used to identify the areas of a picture with the highest contrast. Then, like a magnet, it snaps on the edge between those pieces. Images with a distinct item in the foreground and significant contrast between it and the background—such as a black mountain range against a bright sky—are ideal for using the Magnetic Lasso tool. **Before you start choosing, you may also modify the Magnetic Lasso tool's settings in the Tool Options window:**

+ The width of the Magnetic Lasso tool determines how near you have to move your mouse to the edge (between 1 and 256 pixels) before it clamps to that edge. If there is a lot of detail on the edge or the picture contrast is poor, choose a lower number. For photographs with smoother edges or great contrast, use a higher value.

+ Contrast: You may adjust the Magnetic Lasso's contrast requirement (ranging from 1% to 100%) before it clamps to an edge. Use a larger percentage if the area you want to alter and the backdrop of the picture contrast well.

- It instructs the software on the number of fixing points (ranging from 1 to 100) that should be shown on the selection line. As the value increases, so do the points. Keep the number low if the object you want to choose has a smooth edge. If there is a lot of information on the edge, choose a larger number.
- Tablet Pressure (pen icon): If your drawing tablet is pressure-sensitive, choose this option to increase stylus pressure, which will reduce the edge width.

To utilize the Magnetic Lasso tool, follow these steps:

- The Tools panel has the Magnetic Lasso tool. Choose it. The L key may also be used to switch between the various Lasso tools. The magnetic rope tool has a tiny magnet at the end and resembles a rope with straight sides.
- To position the initial attaching point, click the edge of the item you want to choose. Fastening points hold the selection line in place. Click on the border between the desired portion and the undesirable backdrop. Anywhere is a good place to start.
- Without clicking, keep dragging your pointer over the thing. Only the most recent portion of the selection line remains active, but the fixing points keep it in place. To lock down a fastening point, slide your mouse back and click if the Magnetic Lasso tool begins to stray from the edge of the item you want to pick. Press Backspace (or Delete on a Mac) to remove any snapping points that the Magnetic Lasso tool inserts where you don't want them. Repeatedly using the Delete or Backspace keys removes the fixing points. If the Magnetic Lasso doesn't function, you may use one of the other Lasso tools. To pick the Lasso tool, click the mouse button and drag while holding down Alt (Option on a Mac). To pick the Polygonal Lasso tool, click while holding down Alt (Option on the Mac).
- To end the selection, go back to where you were before and click the mouse button. Your cursor is surrounded by a little circle that indicates that you are at the proper location to stop the selection. Another option is to double-click, which will return the selection to its starting position. The selection boundary appears when the selection is closed.

Using the Magic Wand in Wizardry

One of the first digital picture tools ever created was the Magic Wand tool. Since the early days of Photoshop, when Elements was only a concept, this popular feature has existed. Despite its ease of use, it might be challenging to predict the selection outcomes it will provide. The Magic Wand tool selects a picture when you click within it. This choice was based on the color of the pixel you clicked. If the colors of the other pixels are similar to the one you want to choose, elements add them to the selection. However, it might be challenging to estimate the precise level of resemblance needed for the Magic Wand tool to choose a color. However, that's where the Tolerance setting is useful.

Discussing Tolerance

The Tolerance option determines the range of colors the Magic Wand tool may choose from. **Brightness levels, which range from 0 to 255, are the basis for the color spectrum:**
- Only one color is selected when the tolerance is set to 0.
- All colors or the whole picture are selected when the tolerance is set to 255.

Because the default setting is 32, Elements examines the value of that base color and, when you click on a pixel, selects all pixels whose brightness levels are between 16 levels lighter and 16 levels darker. What happens if a picture has several tones of the same color? It's not really important. To increase the number of pixels in the selection, you may click the Magic Wand many times. The Tolerance level may be raised. On the other hand, if your wand selects too much, you may reduce your Tolerance setting. As you can see from our discussion of tolerance, the Magic Wand tool performs best on images that are dark or have few colors. The ideal picture for the Wand would be a solid black item on a white backdrop. Don't use the wand if the picture has a lot of colors and the piece you wish to modify doesn't stand out greatly from the backdrop.

Using the Wand to select

The Magic Wand tool's Tolerance settings may be changed as follows:
- Select the Magic Wand tool from the Tools menu. It resembles a stick with several stars on the tip. Additionally, you may move between the Magic Wand, Quick Selection, and Selection Brush tools by using the letter A. Alternatively, you may choose the tool you want by first selecting any of the tools in the Tool Options.
- Click anywhere on the element of your choice using the default Tolerance of 32. The pixel you click sets the basic color. With the Pixel Gods on your side, you can choose whatever you desire with a single click. If your decision requires further work, as shown in the top image in the photo below, kindly go to Step 3.
- Change the Tolerance setting in the Tool Options. Should the Magic Wand pick excessively, lower the Tolerance setting. If the wand did not choose enough, increase the value.

While exploring the Tool options, you should be aware of the following additional options:

➢ **Sample All Layers:** The Magic Wand will pick pixels from every visible layer if you have many layers and choose this option. If this option is not used, the tool will only choose pixels from the current layer.

➢ Contiguous: The Magic Wand will only choose adjacent pixels when this option is chosen. For the tool to pick all pixels within the tolerance range—even if they are not next to one another—this option is not required.

➢ Anti-aliasing: Softens the selection's edge by one pixel row.

➢ Refine Edge: Press the button to do so. To smooth out your pick and eliminate any jagged edges, adjust the Smooth slider in the Refine Edge dialog box. The Shift Edge slider may be moved to the left or right to enlarge or reduce the selected region.

✛ Click the element you want once more. Regretfully, the Magic Wand tool is unable to automatically alter your original decision. Your new Tolerance setting is used to make a new selection when the existing one is deselected. If the tolerance setting is still incorrect, you may adjust it once again. Try again, try again.

Changing Your Selections

You may discover how to choose the best option for your Magic Wand, Lasso, or Marquee here. The methods listed here are not the only things you can perform by hand. Additionally, you may create a new selection, add to an existing selection, delete from an existing selection, or draw a line between two existing choices using the four selection buttons on the left side of the Tool Options. Pick your preferred selection tool, click the button that allows you to pick it, and then drag (or click if you're using the Polygonal Lasso or Magic Wand tools).

Intersecting, adding to, and deleting from a selection

Most of what you want can be selected with the help of the Marquee, Lasso, and Magic Wand tools, but you can ensure that you only receive what you want by slightly altering the selection's edge:

- **Add:** If your current selection does not yet include all of the items you want to capture, you must add those portions to the edge. To add anything that is already in a Marquee selection, just drag it around while holding down the Shift key. Use the Polygonal Lasso to move your cursor around the region. Additionally, to move the Magic Wand, click the desired location while holding down the Shift key.

- To add to the selection, you don't have to use the same tool you used to construct it in the first place. Any selection tool that you believe will be effective may be used. For example, many individuals use the Magic Wand first, and then the Lasso tool to improve the appearance.

- **Subtract:** Excessive? Holding down the Alt (or Option) key while moving the marker around the desired pixels will remove those pixels from a selection. Use the Alt (or Option) key to add to a selection. Use the Alt (or Option) key to add to the Magic Wand or Polygonal Lasso.

- **Intersect two choices:** Use your fingers to create a shape. Press Shift+Alt (or Shift+Option on a Mac) and drag using the Lasso or Marquee tools to combine two selections. Press those keys and click rather than drag if you're using the Magic Wand or Polygonal Lasso. Only the region that both options share is now present in your selection.

Preventing key collisions

I tell you, if you want to add anything to a selection, you hit the Shift key. What if you want to create a perfect square by adding to the selection? What if you want to simultaneously draw from the center outward and clear a portion of a selection? You must use the Alt (or Option on a Mac) key for both. What on earth is Elements aware of? **Get your preferred Marquee tool and follow these two guidelines to prevent keyboard collisions:**

- Use Shift and drag to add a square or circular selection. Drag while holding down the mouse button. After a moment, release the Shift key and press it once again. The region you added for selection suddenly becomes a circle or square. Then you have to release the Shift key and the mouse button. Verify that the Normal Aspect option is selected.

- Press Alt (Option on the Mac) and drag to remove from an existing selection while drawing outward from the center. Hold down the mouse button while briefly releasing the Alt (or Option on a Mac) key. Then apply pressure once more. You are now sketching from the center outward. Release the mouse button again, followed by the Alt (or Option on a Mac) key.

You may also utilize the Tool Options' selection buttons.

Using the Selection Brush to Paint

If you like the organic sensation of sketching on a canvas, you will enjoy the Selection Brush. Painting over portions of a picture that you want to pick or over portions that you do not want to select is possible in two techniques. You may create a simple selection using this fantastic tool by first using another tool, such as the Lasso. To improve the selection even more, you may then brush additional pixels into or out of it.

The following is how to choose using the Selection Brush:

- From the Tools panel, choose the Selection Brush. It has an oval form with dots around the end that resembles a paintbrush. To transition between the Magic Wand, Quick Selection, and Selection Brush tools, just hit the A key. You may also choose any of these tools under the Tool Options, and then choose the one you want. There are two modes of operation for this tool: Advanced and Quick.

- **In the Tool Options, choose your Selection Brush preferences. A list of each choice is provided below:**

  - **Mode:** To paint over what you want to pick, click Selection; to paint over what you don't want, select Mask. If you choose Mask mode, you will need to select additional overlay options. A color layer that only shows up on the screen, an overlay flows over your picture to indicate whether areas are protected or not. Additionally, choose an overlay level of 1% to 100%. The accent's red hue may be swapped out for another color. This option might be useful if there is a lot of red in your picture.

  - **Brush Presets Picker:** Select a brush from the preset drop-down list. To add more brushes, choose the preset library you want to utilize by clicking the arrow pointing down to the right of Default Brushes. You may choose the Load Brushes command from the panel menu (the downward-pointing arrow).

  - **Size:** Select a brush size in the range of 1 to 2,500 pixels. You have two options: move the slider or enter the number.

  - **Hardness:** Adjust the brush tip's hardness from 1% to 100%. A crisper, more defined stroke is produced by a sharper tip.

- **Apply paint to the relevant areas:**

  - Paint over the regions you want to pick if your mode is selected. A selection boundary is visible. The selection increases with each stroke. (The Tool Options' Add to Selection button is already selected for you.) If you inadvertently add anything you don't want, just paint over the undesirable area by using the Alt (or Option on a Mac) key. Another option is to click the Subtract from Selection box in the Tool Options. Once you've completed painting what you want, your selection is ready to use.

  - If Mask is selected, paint over the regions you do not want to pick. Your mask will become a selection border if you press the Selection or another tool from the Tool Options or the drop-down list labeled "Selection." Remember that your choice is the exact opposite of what you want. You can view the overlay's color as you paint. The cover area increases with each stroke. A red layer is applied to the picture to conceal the sky and overlay it with another sky. Working in Mask mode allows you to hide or mask the areas of the picture that you do not want altered. Any element activity, such as choosing, altering the hue, or anything else, might be that modification. To remove portions of the covered area, paint again and hit Alt (or Option on a Mac).

✛ The boundary of your selection surrounds the object you don't want when you paint over it in Mask mode. To go where you want to go, choose choose > Inverse.

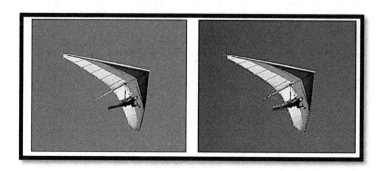

Which mode ought to be selected? You make the decision. One advantage of working in Mask mode is that you may choose certain areas to focus on. Painting with delicate brushes allows you to make decisions with soft edges. Some pixels are only partially picked as a result of these fuzzy edges. Lowering the overlay opacity percentage will further reduce the opaqueness of your pixels. If this seems somewhat similar, it's because it's the same thing that occurs when you feather options.

Using the Quick Selection Tool to Paint

Think of the Quick Selection tool as a Lasso bin, Brush, and Magic Wand all together. The good news is that it is indeed "quick." What's even better is that it's easy to use. The good news? Check it out; the results are rather excellent.

Use this tool to pick fast by doing the following:

✛ From the Tools panel, choose the Quick Selection tool. It is a stick-shaped utensil with a stripe around the end. This tool, the Magic Wand tool, and the Selection Brush tool are all located in the same section of the Tools panel. Additionally, the Magic Wand, Quick Selection, and Selection Brush tools may be switched by pressing the A key. There are two modes of operation for this tool: Advanced and Quick.

✛ **In the Tool choices, provide the choices. A list of the options is shown below:**

➢ **New Selection:** This option, which is the default, allows you to choose something else. You may also add to or subtract from your choices.

➢ **Size:** Select the desired brush size. The width ranges from 1 to 2,500 pixels.

➢ **Brush options:** These options allow you to adjust the brush's roundness, angle, strength, and spacing.

- ➤ **Sample All Layers:** pick this option if you like to pick from every layer in your picture. Only if you leave the current layer deselected will you be able to choose from it.
- ➤ **Auto-Enhance:** If you pick this option, Elements will automatically improve your choices using an algorithm.
- ✦ You may paint or drag the parts of your picture that you choose. Drag expands your options. A portion of the picture becomes part of your selection if you click on it after stopping dragging.
- ✦ **You may add to or remove from your choices as you like:**
  - ➤ To expand your selection, drag the Shift key over the desired regions of the picture while holding it down.
  - ➤ Holding down the Alt (or Option) key, drag it over the area you don't want in your selection to remove it. In the Tool choices, you may also choose the Add to Selection and Subtract from Selection choices.
- ✦ Click the Refine Edge option in the Tool Options and adjust the parameters as needed if you need to fine-tune your pick.

Note: You may even need to use the Lasso or another selection tool to further clean up your item if it has a lot of details. Eventually, you ought to choose something that you're happy with.

Using the Auto Selection Tool for Selection

You may find the selecting tools listed here too challenging. This tool was created just for you. The Auto Selection tool does just what it promises to do: choosing the desired item is fast and easy. This intelligent tool looks at your rough selection and determines what item it believes you want from it based on its understanding of pixels. **Then, it snaps to that thing. Here's how to utilize this awesome tool:**

- ✦ The Tools panel has the Auto Selection tool. Select it. The instrument resembles a wand because of the three little stars on the end. The Tools panel contains the Quick Selection, Selection Brush, and Magic Wand tools. To switch between these tools, you may also use the A key. Note that the New Selection option is automatically highlighted. This utility may be used in either Quick or Advanced mode.

- In the Tool Options, pick the tool you want to use to make your first choice. You may choose from the Rectangular and Elliptical Marquee tools or the Lasso and Polygonal Lasso tools.
- **Additional settings may be configured in the Tool settings:**
  - ➢ **Sample All Layers:** pick this option if you like to pick from every layer in your picture. Only if you leave the current layer deselected will you be able to choose from it.
  - ➢ **Constrain Selection:** This option will maintain the precise square or circular shape of your marquee choices.
- Around the target item in your picture, make a rough selection. I chose the female using the Lasso tool, as shown in the picture below. After making a selection, Elements examines the pixels and instantly snaps to the item you selected when you release the mouse button.
- **As necessary, add to or delete from your choices.**
  - ➢ To expand your selection, drag the desired regions of the picture while holding down the Shift key.
  - ➢ To remove anything from your selection, drag it over the region you don't want while holding down the Alt key (or the Option key on a Mac). In the Tool choices, you may also choose the Add to Selection and Subtract from Selection choices.
- Click the Tool Options' Refine Edge option and adjust the parameters if necessary to fine-tune your pick.

The Background Changer Guided Edit is a must-try if you believe the Auto Selection tool is revolutionary. You may alter or even create your own backdrop using this edit, which is located under the Special Edits in Guided mode.

Using One-Click Selection to Choose Your Subject, Background, or Sky

One of the most frequent queries Adobe receives from users of its software is, "How can I select things more easily and more accurately?" Adobe listened to the pleas and provided two more methods for choosing. **The three one-click selection instructions may be used as follows:**

- Choose Select > Subject or Background or Sky in either Advanced or Quick mode. Additionally, you may click on the Select Subject, Sky, or Background icon keys using the Tool Options of the Quick Selection, Selection Brush, Magic Wand, Refine Selection, and Auto Selection Tools.
- You may add to or delete from your selection using any of the selection tools if you need to tidy it up after Step 1. The Lasso tool is located under the Auto Selection Tool's Tool Options. We like it best for minor cleanups.
  - ➢ To expand your selection, drag the desired regions of the picture while holding down the Shift key.
  - ➢ To remove anything from your selection, drag it over the region you don't want while holding down the Alt key (or the Option key on a Mac). In the Tool choices, you may also choose the Add to Selection and Subtract from Selection choices.
- To improve your choice even more, use the "Refine Edge" option from the Tool Options. After that, change the settings as necessary.

Using the Refine Selection Brush to Adjust

Making rapid and accurate decisions is a highly sought-after talent. Fortunately, Elements comes with an additional tool that makes learning this ability simple. By automatically recognizing the boundaries of your chosen element, the Refine Selection Brush assists you in adding or removing elements of your selection.

You may choose from the following options using this tool:

- Use the Selection Brush, Quick Selection tool, or any other selection tool to make your choice. Elements doesn't care how you make your initial choice, provided you have one. If it's not flawless, that's acceptable. Thus, in this instance, the Refine Selection Brush is helpful.

- The Refine Selection Brush should be selected. This tool is located in the same tool location as the Quick Selection, Magic Wand, Selection Brush, and Smart Selection tools. Your pointer seems to be two overlapping circles. The outer circle represents the environment in which Tolerance finds an edge.

- **Adjust the parameters under the Tool Options. The choices you have are described by these words:**

  - **Size:** You may adjust your brush's size by dragging the slider between 1 and 2,500 pixels.

  - **Snap Strength:** You may adjust the snap strength from 0% to 100% using the slider. Snap Strength indicates the force of the pull.

  - **Selection Edge:** You may adjust the edge's hardness or softness using the slider. You may be able to acquire the desired option if you move the slider closer to soft if your item has wispier edges, such as hair, fur, or feathers. Setting your mode to "Add" and holding down the mouse button on the item will increase the size of the selection within your concentric rings. The selection edge, which is the lighter region around your center circle, enlarges. This region displays your object's edge. Make sure this is where your whole advantage is. Remember that you may also "paint" the edge using the Refine Selection Brush tool. It could take some experimenting and adjusting the settings to achieve the choice you want if the item is complex. However, if you persist, you ought to get the desired detail.

  - **Add/Subtract:** You may increase or decrease your choices if you pick this option.

  - **Push:** "Push" refers to moving your cursor within the selection to enlarge it inside the cursor's outer circle. The pointer will snap to a part's edge if you move it near to it. Your cursor will shrink until it fits within the outer circle if you move it outside of the selection.

  - **Smooth:** Use this setting to smooth down the edge of your selection if it seems a little jagged.

  - **View:** To see the selection, choose a view option. You may see the item of your choice against a black or white backdrop. To see it with a crimson, somewhat see-through overlay on top of it, choose Overlay. Remember that the layer option allows you to adjust the layer's transparency.

- To make your choice even better till you're satisfied, use the Refine Selection Brush. A picture of the final choice may be seen below.

The Cookie Cutter Tool in Use

The Cookie Cutter tool has a funny name and is a powerful instrument. It may be thought of as the Custom Shape tool in an image format. However, the Custom form tool just uses a mask to conceal anything outside the form, but the Cookie Cutter tool removes everything outside the shape. The preconfigured libraries include a variety of interesting shapes, such as Swiss cheese and conversation bubbles. (Look at the food library; we're serious.)

The following is a guide on using the Cookie Cutter:

- From the Tools panel, choose the Cookie Cutter tool. It is impossible to overlook this flower-shaped gadget. The C key may also be pressed. Next to each other are the Cookie Cutter and the two Crop tools. If it's not visible, press C until it appears, or choose the Crop tool from the Tool Options and then the Cookie Cutter.

- **In the Tool Options, choose your desired action. The list is as follows:**
  - ➢ **Shape**: Select a shape from the Custom Shape options library. Click the Shapes menu and choose a library from the list that displays if you want to load another one. You may draw a form with specific bounds using the geometry options.
  - ➢ **Unrestricted:** With this option, you can draw whatever you want.
  - ➢ **Defined Proportions:** This feature allows you to maintain the proper ratios of width to height. The picture may be cropped to the original, fixed size of the form you choose using "Defined Size." However, the image's size cannot be altered.
  - ➢ **Fixed Size:** You may choose the desired width and height using this option. The "From Center" option allows you to draw the form from the center outward.
  - ➢ Feather: This option creates a soft-edged selection.
  - ➢ **Crop:** By selecting "Crop," the picture will be cropped into the desired form. Place the form within the image window.

- To build the form you want, drag your mouse over the picture. Then, size the shape by moving one of the bounding box's handles. Finally, position the shape by dragging the mouse pointer within the box. Other transformations, such as skewing and rotation, may also occur. These functions may be accessed by manually dragging the box or by inputting numbers in the Tool Options.
- To complete the cutout, click the image's Commit button or hit Enter. In the picture below, the image has been sliced into the form of a leaf. To exit the bounding box without erasing the picture, you may always click the "Cancel" button or hit Esc.

Using the Eraser Tools to Eliminate

You may use the Eraser tools to delete portions of your picture. The Background Eraser, Magic Eraser, and Standard Eraser are its three eraser tools. Since the Eraser tools resemble the pink erasers you used in primary school, it is impossible to overlook them. If you are unable to locate the three tools, you may always hit E to move between them. Pixels are eliminated when they are removed. Before using the Eraser tools, make sure you have a duplicate of your picture saved elsewhere. It functions similarly to inexpensive insurance in the event of an emergency.

The tool for Erasing

As seen here, you may use the Eraser tool to erase portions of your picture to your backdrop color or, if you're working on a layer, a transparent background.

All you have to do is choose this tool and move it over the desired section of the picture. It's not the most exact tool in the world, so use tiny brush tips and zoom in close to obtain a nice wipe.

There are many Eraser choices available under the Tool choices:

- **Brush Presets Picker:** Click the drop-down menu to access the Brush presets. Select a brush. Again, the Brush list has other brush sets. (Press the downward pointing arrow in the top right corner.)
- **Size:** Select a brush size from 1 to 2,500 pixels by moving the Size tool. The bracket keys on the left and right may be used to adjust the brush's size.
- **Opacity:** Select a transparency percentage for the areas you want to remove. Lowering the Opacity option reduces the amount of data that is deleted. You can't utilize opacity in Block mode.
- **Type:** Select Block, Pencil, or Brush. When you pick Block, you are only able to select one size (a 16x16-pixel tip) and are not able to select any other fixed brushes.

The tool for background erasing

The backdrop Eraser tool, which is more intelligent than the Eraser tool, removes an image's backdrop while taking care to preserve the foreground. You may make a layer translucent by erasing it using the Background Eraser tool. Elements immediately converts the background into a layer when you use this tool to a picture that simply contains a backdrop. Keep the "hot spot," or the crosshair in the center of the brush, on the background pixels when you move the Background Eraser. The hot spot captures and eliminates the color of a pixel when it crosses the border of the brush. However, it is also deleted if you accidentally touch a foreground pixel with the hot spot. Even the tool feels no remorse for its actions! Images with strong color contrast between the foreground and background items are ideal for making the most of this tool. If your picture has wispy or highly detailed edges (such as hair or fur), layer masking may also provide good results.

All of the Background Eraser options are listed here:

- **Brush Settings:** To manipulate the brush tip's Size, Hardness, Spacing, Roundness, and Angle, click the Brush Settings button. For drawing tools that react to pressure, set the Size and Tolerance at the bottom.

- **Restrictions:** Discontiguous eliminates all pixels of the same color, regardless of their location within the picture. Contiguous erases any pixels of the same hue that are adjacent to those underneath the hot spot.
- **Tolerance:** This figure indicates to Elements how near the color underneath the hot spot the colors must be before being erased. When the value is greater, it detects more colors; when the value is lower, it detects fewer colors.

The tool called Magic Eraser

The Eraser and Magic Wand tools may be combined to create the Magic Eraser tool. It simultaneously selects and removes pixels of the same color. Pixels are wiped to transparency while working on a layer that does not have transparency locked. If you're working on a picture with only a backdrop, Elements transforms the background into a layer. **While there are a few settings that set the Magic Eraser apart from the others, the most of the options are the same:**
- **Sample All levels:** This method only removes pixels on the active layer, but it samples colors from all visible levels.
- **Contiguous:** Selects and eliminates every pixel next to the hot area that has the same color.
- **Anti-aliasing:** Softens the edges of the transparent region.

Making Use of the Select Menu

By expanding, contracting, smoothing, softening, rotating, and capturing pixels of the same hue, you may further alter your options using this menu. If it doesn't satisfy your selection demands, nothing else will.

Selecting everything or nothing

The Select All and Deselect instructions are easy to understand. To select every element in your picture, pick Select > All or use Ctrl+A (or cmd+A on a Mac). To remove all selections, choose Select > De Select or hit Ctrl+D (or cmd+D on a Mac). Remember that selecting all isn't always necessary. Elements assumes that you can alter the whole picture when there is no selection boundary around it.

A selection being reselected

To avoid losing their selection before they can go on to the next thing, people give up their second cup of coffee to stabilize their palm and carefully lasso around the item they wish to capture. However, you may remove your selection if you accidentally click your mouse while the selection line is still active. Fortunately for us, Elements anticipated this issue and includes a workaround: selecting Select → Reselect will restore your previous choices. The Reselect command only applies to the last selection you made, so bear that in mind. You will not be allowed to reselect if you make a selection after the one you want to reselect. If you save a selection, you can use it again.

Reversing a selection

An ancient song once said, "Love the one you're with if you can't be with the one you love." It kind of explains how Elements' selecting process works. Choosing what you don't want is simpler than choosing what you do. For example, it could be easier to use the Magic Wand to click on the studio backdrop and then choose select → Inverse to turn the selection around if you want to pick out your boyfriend in his senior photo.

Selecting a feather

I demonstrated how to feather a selection created with the Lasso and Marquee tools by putting a number in the Feather box in the Tool Options. If you choose to utilize this method of feathering, keep in mind that you must first set the feather value. I neglected to clarify that you may add a feather after you've made your choice. Select "Feather" and enter any desired value between 0.2 and 250 pixels. After then, your selection's edges are softer. This is the most effective method. Make your choice and then refine it using the methods I described before. Next, put on your feather. It becomes difficult to alter your first option if you use the feather before choosing one. The marquee outline of the selection adjusts to match the feathering when you utilize it to create a selection. Because the marquee outline doesn't precisely accompany your mouse movement, it's more difficult to modify that pick.

Sharpening a selection's edges

The Refine Edge option allows you to adjust the edges of your selection. It's not how you obtained it that counts, but the choice. The command is located in the Tool Options of the Magic Wand, Lasso, and Quick Selection tools. It's also available on the Select menu. **What you need know about each of this button's settings is as follows:**

+ **See Mode:** Select a mode from the menu that displays to see your choices in a different manner. Move your cursor over each setting to get a description. Marching Ants, for instance, demonstrates the selection's edge. With overlay, you may preview how your selection will appear with the borders obscured and a somewhat translucent layer of color in the unchosen region. The pick stands up on a black or white backdrop thanks to On Black and On White. Instead of displaying a preview of the selection, this button displays the actual picture. The Show Radius indicates the size of the region where edge polishing is occurring.
+ **Smart Radius:** Elements will adjust the radius for both soft and hard edges that are at the edge of your selection if you pick this option. If the hardness or softness of your border is consistent, you may want to avoid using this option. The radius setting may now be adjusted more precisely.
+ **Radius:** This indicates the size of the selection border upon refinement. To improve the edges in areas with soft edges or a lot of detail, raise the radius. Look at your pick and tweak the slider to find a decent setting.
+ **Smooth:** Reduces the sharpness of your selection's edges.

195

- To make an edge softer and more blurry, feather it by moving the tool to the right.
- **Contrast:** Raising the contrast reduces line fuzziness and eliminates artifacts. Try the Smart Radius option before experimenting with Contrast.
- **Shift Edge:** Changes the size of the selected region. You may aid in defringing (removing extraneous background pixels) the boundaries of your selection by significantly lowering the selection border.
- **Decontaminate Colors:** This option applies the chosen element's colors to the background fringe. Because decontamination alters the colors of certain pixels, you will need to export to or create a new layer or document in order to preserve your current layer. To see the cleaning process, choose Reveal Layer as your View mode.
- **Amount:** This modifies the air's cleanliness.
- **Output To:** Select the location where your cleaned and enhanced selection should be saved. You have the option to save it to a new document, a layer mask, a layer, a layer with a layer mask, or your current layer.
- **Refine Radius tool:** Select the Paintbrush tool from the menu on the left and paint around the image's edge to alter the region you're polishing. To observe the precise region that is being included or excluded, switch to Marching Ants as your View mode. By shifting the right and left boxes, you may adjust the brush's size.
- You may use the Erase Refinements tool, which is located on the left and resembles an eraser, to remove any adjustments you didn't want to make using the Refine Radius tool.
- **Zoom tool:** To see how your settings are mirrored, zoom in on your picture.
- **Hand tool:** This allows you to manipulate the picture window to see how your selections alter the situation.

Making use of the Modify commands

Although the Modify submenu's instructions aren't very well-liked, they might sometimes be helpful. **Everything you need know about every command:**

- **Boundary:** When you pick "Border," a region around the selection boundary that is between 1 and 200 pixels is selected. To apply color to the border, choose Edit > Fill Selection.
- **Smooth:** Removes any sharp, uneven edges. You may choose from 1 to 100 pixels. Based on the quantity you specified, Elements will next examine each chosen pixel and determine whether to add or delete it from your selection. Begin with a little quantity, such as one, two, or three pixels. If you don't, your choice may be less accurate.
- The "Expand" option allows you to enlarge your selection by a certain amount of pixels, ranging from 1 to 100. This command is especially useful if you narrowly missed obtaining the edge of an elliptical selection and need to enlarge it a little.
- **Contract:** Trims your selection's edge by 1 to 100 pixels. You may find it useful to slightly reduce the size of your selection if you want to apply a feather when combining many photos. In this manner, you may avoid picking up background pixels at the margins of your selection.

Using the commands Grow and Similar

The Grow and Similar directives are often used in conjunction with the Magic Wand tool. Try choosing Click, Select, and then Grow if your first Magic Wand option wasn't precisely what you expected. The selection that falls within the tolerance range is enlarged by the Grow command, which adds pixels adjacent to it. Similar to Grow, the Similar command has the ability to choose pixels that are not next to one another. The command scans the picture, picking up pixels that fall inside the Tolerance range. The tolerance for these remarks cannot be altered. The Tolerance value may be seen in the Tool Options when you choose the Magic Wand tool. The Tolerance setting may be adjusted to display a greater or lesser number of colors.

Selections are saved and loaded

If you spend too much time on a challenging pick, you may want to put it off until later. Saving it is not only feasible, but also wise. It's also rather simple. How to accomplish it:

- When you're finished modifying your selection, pick pick >Save Selection.
- Give your selection a name and leave the Selection option set to New Selection when the Save Selection dialog box appears. Automatically, the procedure is set to New Selection.
- Click OK.
- To return to the selection, click select > Load Selection and select an item from the drop-down menu.

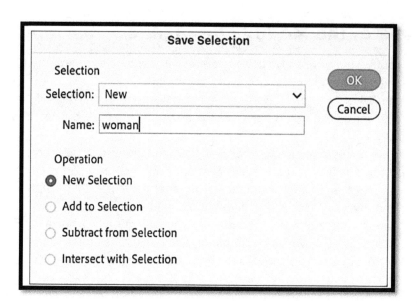

CHAPTER FIFTEEN
ABOUT HINTS AND METHODS

How to make a backup of your catalog

The importance of backing up hard drives and the priceless data that they have spent hours developing and updating is something that most computer users discover the hard way. Don't spend any more time editing your photos with Elements. Right now, we can save you the bother. It's time to back-up your data when you've been working on a project for a long time and it would be difficult to start again. Generally speaking, this is the norm. Always create a duplicate of the catalog file before organizing your files, adding keyword tags, creating albums, stacks, and version sets. This is due to the possibility of harm to the catalog file. It's fantastic that users of both Mac and Windows operating systems may use the catalog backup function. Creating a backup on a USB device with a 1 terabyte capacity will provide the greatest results.

Use Elements to back-up your catalog by doing the following:

- To access the Backup Catalog Wizard, choose File→Backup Catalog. Elements' two-panel interface will guide you through the hassle-free process of creating a backup of your data.

- Select the source you want to support. You have the following choices in the Backup Catalog to Hard Drive Wizard's first pane:

  - **Catalog-only Backup:** Only the keywords and tags are kept if you merely backup the catalog. Places, events, phrases, tags, and more are all included in a complete backup. It is also possible to back up pictures and films. If you have a big collection with plenty of pictures and movies, creating a backup will take a long time. If you don't need to back-up your images and videos, you may choose this option. In other words, everything except the pictures and videos will be backed up with this choice. Compared to the complete copy, this alternative is far quicker.

  - **Full Back-up:** If you want to back-up everything, including your images and movies, this is the option to choose.

  - **Incremental Backup:** Choose this option if you have already performed at least one backup and want to modify the files that were backed up.

- Choose a destination location for your backed-up files by clicking Next. The "Select Destination Drive" list is the list of drives that your computer is now using. It consists of live disks; external hard drives connected to your computer, and mounted network devices. After you choose a drive, Elements will immediately assess the write speed and locate any previous backup files that may have been created. A list of all the files that need copying, together with their sizes, is provided by the wizard. This information is useful because it indicates if a backup drive has sufficient capacity to complete the backup or whether the backup requires many disks to complete (in the case of Windows).

- After selecting Browse, enter the location where the files must go. You may use this to transfer files to your computer's hard disk or to another hard drive that is connected to it.
- Click "Save Backup" to save the backup. The backup restarts. Make sure there are no obstacles preventing the backup from continuing. You should just wait for Elements to complete its job until you hear that it's finished since the backup might take some time.

How to create a file and picture backup

It would take a long time to manually transfer files from your first hard disk to a second hard drive, CD, or DVD. Finding evidence to support it with elements is simple. From the menu, choose File > Copy/Move to Removable Drive. In the following window, check the box next to Copy Files and click following. Click OK after selecting a disk and giving the backup folder a name. It makes a backup copy of every file you view in the Organizer.

Advice and Techniques for Effective Editing

Construct a Photo Calendar

A calendar would make a wonderful present for friends, family, and coworkers. Better yet, it's an enjoyable method to practice shooting. Additionally, creating a calendar is really simple. Adobe has simplified some really difficult-to-understand image changes into a straightforward one-click procedure in this instance. It functions quite well overall.

- You may organize your work and create a book for your calendar photos in the Extra Tools and Features section. This is an excellent concept for the majority of Elements art projects.
- The Organizer's top right corner has the Create drop-down menu. From that option, choose Photo Calendar. A number of calendar types are shown in the next phase.
- Select an artistic style.

A tip: Make sure the "Auto Fill with Selected Images" box is not selected, then choose one of the 31 styles offered, input the start month and year, and click "OK." After that, placing the appropriate images on the appropriate pages is easy. You may have to wait while Adobe sends you the templates for that style.

- If the front cover isn't there already, start by going to the main screen. You can locate the calendar's accompanying photos in the Photo Bin at the foot of each page if you save them in an album. To utilize an image, click and hold it, then move it into one of the gray areas. To match the curvature of the picture frame, the calendar design automatically rotates and changes size.

+ Type your title and description in the text box that appears when you double-click. Verify your writing by clicking the green "OK" button. If there are errors, return to the page, double-click the text to bring it up again, and correct it.

+ Repeat the process of clicking, holding, and pushing for the remaining monthly images.

+ **Customize:** You can easily change how many photographs are on a page or how they are arranged using the Layouts tab in the Advanced or Basic window.

+ To switch up the style, double-click the image when you reach the screen. It's simple. You may use one or all of them for this. That's more than you can learn from this class. You may learn how to modify each layer's characteristics independently in Advanced mode.

+ When you're finished, save the calendar file so that it can be printed. This may be made using a standard photo inkjet printer. In addition to the cover, there are twelve pages. After that, you may get it wrapped in spiral paper at an office supply store. It is now prepared for sending to loved ones.

Design a greeting card

The processes for creating a calendar and a welcome card are almost identical. The one distinction is that you just have to create one page rather than twelve.

The location and size of the images in the menu may be altered.

+ It's simple to make a Christmas card. Simply place a few photos in an organizer album.

+ Select one, two, or three images from this album if you would like several images on the card. Next, from the Create menu, choose Greeting Card.

+ One of the minor design choices will appear. Pick one of their styles. Then click OK. You may click or drag an image from the Photo Bin into the card art after it has finished downloading. Look closely at the options on the right side of the Greeting Card page. Both the design style and the quantity of images utilized are modifiable.

Workplace advice

One of my problems with this tool is that it is only designed to be used for writing on one side. This is probably due to the fact that not everyone has a dual-sided inkjet printer at home. **Additionally, the majority of the designs resemble flyers rather than cards.**

- As I've previously said, I believe the little window displaying the various card kinds is outdated. For this reason, I believe that making your cards by hand is preferable.
- If I were to use it, I would place one or two photographs on the bottom side of this. When it is made and folded in half, the image will be on the front and the back will be blank.
- Use matte paper for printing. Not only does it have fantastic color, it's also easy to score flat and fold. Although this kind of glossy paper feels nicer and is thicker, it is more difficult to fold correctly.
- Before folding the card, cut the spine with a dull knife or use a card bending tool, which is often available at a craft shop.

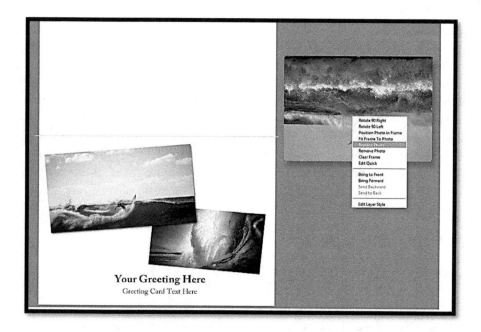

- After downloading the chosen design, rearrange the images on the card to see whether you accidentally placed them there. To do this, right-click on the image, choose Replace Photo or Delete, and then locate another image.
- Place the image stands in the finest possible location. When printing them at home, take note of the yellow line in the center. When there are images in the center of a page, it might be challenging to fold it in half. I used the shift tool to shift the other two below the center line and discarded the one at the top.

The double-headed arrow turns into a spinning arrow as you move the mouse near the margins of an image. In other words, you may adjust the picture's rotation by clicking, holding, and dragging it. Click the green "check" button after making changes to your photo to ensure everything was done correctly. Conserve. One of these projects makes a difference when you save it. pse file format. Text, images, clip art, and color may all be stored in this kind of file. Only PSE files may open in Elements; PSD files cannot. The only way to save this is as a PDF file, which is accessible to everybody.

Make a Photo Collage

In both the Editor and the Organizer, the Create button is located in the upper left corner of the screen. It enables you to include your images on elegant pages that can be sent as digital files or printed. Elements offers a large selection of pre-made designs. To create projects that are uniquely yours, you may alter every aspect of them. You may use images to create a collage page in Create. This kind of page might feature one or more images or a backdrop with a theme. Elements immediately provides you with a basic layout along with recommendations for photo locations. The backdrop, frame styles, and other elements may be altered. Additionally, you may add or delete pictures.

To assemble a collage of photographs:

- Choose a few images in the Organizer or open them in the Editor. This is a choice, however if you choose the images in advance, Elements will immediately add them to the collage.

Take note: If you change photos and forget to save them, Elements will notify you that all of your open files will be saved immediately before creating your collage. After you've finished making modifications you don't want to retain, close the files and begin a new project called Create.

- Select the Create→Photo Collage option. Elements will lead you to the Editor once you begin creating the collage in the Organizer. At first glance, the Photo Collage window seems tiny, but don't let that deter you. You'll return to the main Editor window after selecting your option and clicking OK.
- Select a page size from the menu on the left side of the Photo Collage window. You may print this project at home if you're unsure what "Print locally" (above the size selections) implies. "Shutterfly" will appear above the products you may purchase from them on some of the other projects, such as picture books that you can print online.

Advice: It may be simpler to start again with a fresh file in Advanced mode if you begin a collage and are unhappy with the route you choose. This is due to the inability to fast switch between portrait and landscape collage sizes. Everything that you can accomplish here, you can do there. The only distinction is that you don't begin with a preconceived project. You must add anything you want to include rather than altering what is already there.

- In the Photo Collage window's center, choose a theme. You may match the backgrounds and frames to your photos with several themes. You may even match the text styles with certain themes. You can see your options more clearly on the right side of the window when you click on the image of a theme to choose it. You can alter any aspect of the Create window, even if you don't like any of the pre-existing styles. Select the theme that you are less fond of.

Keep in mind: If you begin your first collage with the Basic theme, you may not see any further choices. Alright, no problem. It's simple to remove any superfluous frames in step 7.

- Give Elements the option to add your photos to the collage automatically. The "Autofill with Selected Images" option at the bottom of the Photo Collage window should not be unchecked. When Elements creates the collage, the images you selected in Step 1 will be inserted right away from the Organizer or Photo Bin. If you didn't choose a photo in advance, the Editor will use the one that is now selected. Don't tick this option if you want to choose which shots go where.

- Click OK after you've made your choices. Elements returns you to the main Create window, where you begin creating the collage. The collage is shown in the area that you may alter. Elements will frame the images for you if you choose them in advance and leave the Autofill option selected. Every image in the collage gets its appearance from the layer. If you didn't choose any photographs (or enough to fill all the places), you may see the phrases "Click here to add photo or Drag photo here" in each empty frame. It's okay if you include images in step 8. At this point, we may operate in what Adobe refers to as "Basic mode."

- Select a layout. After it has completed making the collage, Elements will provide you additional choices. Below the "Create" box is a button labeled "Pages." Clicking this button causes the collage's one page image to appear automatically. The project may consist of several pages, similar to a picture book. This is where you would flip between each page's images. You don't have to make any changes if you like the example that Elements provides. Below the Create screen comes the Layouts button. Upon clicking on it, what will happen? You can see a list of the many types according on how many images they can save. Double-click or drag its image into the collage in the viewing area to test out an alternative strategy. Try a different one and erase it (Ctrl+Z/⌘-Z) if you don't like it.

One tip is to scroll down the Create panel until you find a layout with just one or two photographs if you only want to utilize a small number of them. This will immediately eliminate the superfluous photo frames in the Basic layout. Double-clicking will remove the excess frames.

- Modify the pictures. If you haven't already, you may drag an image from the Photo Bin to the frame. If the Photo Bin is not visible, click the "Photo Bin" button under the sample area. You may also click on the blank collage frame with text on it to open a selection box where you can choose an image. Regardless of the method you used, you may make several changes to the collage's images once you've added them. The following adjustments are easy to make:

  ➢ When you click on a frame, the box for the Move tool should appear around it. Click the "Tool Options" box underneath the sample area to see the Move Tool's choices. You can use the Move tool to spread out or match your photographs by stacking them in the proper sequence.

  ➢ Choose the frame you want to alter in style by clicking the Graphics button under the Create panel. Next, double-click or drag the desired frame onto the panel's image.

- Make the collage your own. Click on an image and drag it to a new location in your collage. The Graphics button is located next to the Create panel. After clicking it, drag the panel's artwork into your collage. No matter what size you choose, these images will still look fantastic. By selecting the T on the left side of the viewing area and then clicking the desired location, you may also add text. You may apply effects to the whole page and smooth out your image by switching to Advanced mode.
- **Complete your collage. After you're done, you may choose from the following:**
  - ➢ In the Create section, click Save at the bottom. By doing this, the Save As box will open, allowing you to name the project and save it. Only Create projects may utilize this kind of file. Either a PDF or a PSE file must be saved. However, you may click Close at the bottom of the Create section if you decide you don't like your collage. Then, when Elements asks you to save your work, don't. To create a collage in a common image format, such as a TIFF or JPEG, follow these instructions. Share your collage after that. When you're finished, you may save your collage, but to ensure that you don't lose anything in the event of a computer crash, you may wish to click "Save" often while working.
  - ➢ You may print your image from Create just like any other file. To print, click the Print button at the bottom of the Elements window or press Ctrl+P or ⌘+P.
  - ➢ You may share your photo with others who are unable to access PSE files or send it to a service that can only print JPEG files. After that, choose Export Creations under File. In the new window that appears, you may save your picture as a JPEG, TIFF, or PDF file. From the drop-down box, choose the desired kind. Next, choose the location for saving it by clicking Browse.

Modifying Pictures and Frames

With Elements, you may alter a collage's images in a variety of ways:
Rotate the picture inside its frame. Rotate 90 Left or Rotate 90 Right may be selected by right-clicking or control-clicking on an image. **The image will rotate 90 degrees either clockwise or counterclockwise as a result.**
- Modify how a picture looks in its frame. The "Position Photo in Frame" option will appear when you RMB or control-click a photo.
- Take a picture out of the collage. To remove the emptiness and frame around the image, click on it and then hit Backspace or Delete. Alternatively, right-click or hold on the image and choose "Clear Photo."
- Take a picture and remove a frame. Holding down the image or doing a right-click will allow you to choose "Clear Frame."
- Resize a frame. Before or after a photo is inserted, the size of the frame may be altered. To display the adjustment handles, hold down the mouse button on a blank section of the frame (not the temporary text). Then, drag a corner handle to adjust the frame's size. You can also turn frames using these handles.
- To fit a picture, resize a frame. To make the frame fit the photo rather than the other way around, click or hold on the image and choose "Fit Frame To Photo."

- Modify an image. Elements will immediately transfer the image to "Quick Fix" so you can make any last-minute adjustments if you press and hold the image and choose "Edit Quick." In some file formats, this phrase is grayed out for some reason. However, it is ineffective for collages. In the upper left corner of the preview window is the "Back to Creations" button. Click it once the modifications have been made.
- Include one more picture. From the Create panel's Graphics section, drag a frame to a collage blank. To add a photo, click within the frame. To view it, you may need to click Graphics underneath the text line. If you approach the new frame too closely, it may replace the old one. To reverse what you just accomplished, do not hit Ctrl+Z or Cmd-Z. Next, gently move it to the vacant area once again. You may also drag an image into the frame from the Photo Bin.
- Modify a frame's layer style. Layer styles are now included in the majority of the frames in the Create panel. You may alter the layer's style by performing a right-click on a frame inside the picture. This allows you to adjust things like the drop shadow size of the frame.
- To improve a picture, use a filter. You may rapidly make items seem brushed or rubber-stamped by using the several effects available in "Advanced" mode. However, you must simplify the layer before you can apply effects to the image.

Generate a Photo Book

With the help of elements, you can create pages in various sizes for picture books that you can print off and give as presents. To get started, select Create and then Photo Book. There are many sizes available to you. Sizes are shown on the left side of the Photo Book window. Clicking on one cause the details about that size to update on the right, as shown below. The majority of photo books are purchased online, but you can print an 8.5-by-11-inch (really, 11-by-8.5-inch) photo book at home. Any Create creation may be printed at home if you'd like.

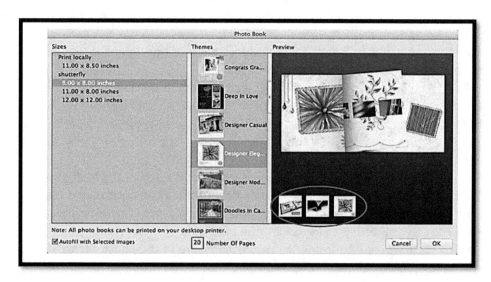

You may choose how many pages you want in the box at the bottom of the photo book. If you know how long you want the book to be, this is helpful. Since 20 pages is the smallest size available, Shutterfly photo albums begin with that. You cannot remove pages to reduce the total to fewer than 20 since Shutterfly will only create 100 pages including the title page. Select the "Print locally" option for an 11" x 8.5" book if you wish to create a 4- or 10-page book. The number in the box at the bottom of the Photo Book window may change at some point, so keep that in mind. The smallest number of pages required to create picture books might be altered by Shutterfly. Making a picture book is similar to making a collage. The sole change is that you may now browse between the pages in the Pages panel in the Create section. Click the Pages button under the Create panel to see it. To begin working on a different two-page spread, just click on it. Use the buttons above the empty area to navigate between pages. The double-page spreads that appear when you open the book are visible.

Keep in mind: The first page is the title page since most picture books don't have a front cover. Click on the image of the two-page spread you want to duplicate in the Pages section. The page will be added to your picture book as a result. Next, choose "Add Page" from the menu at the top of the screen. One page of a two-page spread cannot be eliminated. To get rid of it, click the trash can button after clicking on its image. Be careful not to print fewer pages than the required amount while using Shutterfly. By moving the pages' images on the panel, you may rearrange the pages. Similar to creating a collage, after you're finished creating the book, you can click Save or Print at the bottom of the Elements box. You may also purchase the book on Shutterfly instantly if you choose one of their choices in the Photo Book box. Below the location where you can see it is a "buy" button. The document may be saved as a PDF, which is widely compatible. Then purchase the book from another publisher. Click "Save" to save a picture book. Select the Photo Project Format (PSE) option if you want to alter the book at a later time. You have the option to save it as a PDF after you've finished editing it. Another option is to click the Export button. Photo book files in the Photo Bin and Organizer feature an icon that resembles a pile of pages. It used to be possible to access it and see individual pages. You can't do that now.

Hint: You may create a book of images without using Elements' Photo Book feature. All you need to do now is open your browser, go to Shutterfly.com, and upload your images. The company will then publish them in its picture book format. This technique is applicable to Lulu.com, MyPublisher.com, and other photo-printing websites. Mac users may purchase books using iPhoto and, when it launches, the new Photos program.

Construct a Photo Reel

- Choose the pictures you want to use for the Photo Reel by going to File > Open.

Note: A minimum of two images are required to create a Photo Reel.

- In the "Create" menu, choose "Photo Reel."
- The Timeline will display the frames for each of the selected images. The photographs may be moved around by dragging and dropping them.

Keep in mind: The Layout panel has more photo selections. Select the "Add media from the computer or organizer" option to add other images.

- In the Layout section, you may choose a picture arrangement that complements the social network you want to utilize. Instagram, Facebook, YouTube, TikTok, Snapchat, Twitter, and Threads all have common layouts available in the Layout box.

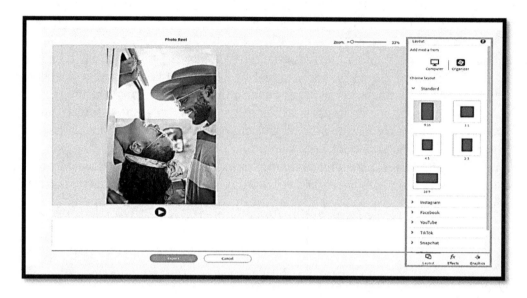

In the image reel, every frame depicts a distinct period. You may adjust this by tapping on the time shown in the picture clip. The time will appear consistently across all of your images if you tick the option next to Apply to All. Click the three-dot button above the images to change further parameters for each frame. The Type tool lets you add the text you desire to your photos. To suit your demands, you may also alter the text's font, size, style, color, heading, tracking, alignment, and other elements.

To get the desired impact in your photos, use one of the following actions:

- Select the desired Effects image, and then apply it just to that image.
- Selecting "Apply to all photos" will alter the appearance of every single one of them.
- Select "No Effect" to reverse the previous action.

Note: The Effects panel's strength slider allows you to adjust the effects' intensity.

- To choose the drawing you want to use, click on any image in the drawings section.
- To export the Photo Reel as an MP4 or GIF file, choose Export > export.

Construct a Print Quote

There are three options: choose an image from the Organizer, open an image in the Photo Editor, or begin without selecting an image. You may use the Create drop-down menu from either the Organizer or the Photo Editor. From there, choose Quote Graphic. The first screen displays the designs from which you may choose. You may start from scratch and avoid using a design if you choose this option.

Select a template to use. The screen immediately shifts to display a list of shared locations and configured sizes. Among other things, you may create a Pinterest post, a Facebook cover, an Instagram post, or a Twitter tweet. You may open it in the Photo Editor at one of the preset sizes if you don't want to share it on social media.

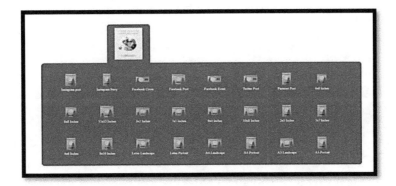

The Background/Effects panel appears after selecting an option in the second panel. The backdrop panel, where you may choose from a variety of backdrop patterns and hues, is the default. You have access to a vast array of effects when you click on the Effects panel. The panel displays the default image as shown. Drag a new image into the document from the Photo Editor's Photo Bin. When you are finished, click the Save button located at the bottom of the Background and Effects boxes.

CHAPTER SIXTEEN
ABOUT SHARING, EXPORTING, AND OUTPUT

Making Use of the Share Panel

One of two interfaces will appear if you click on one of the buttons in the Share panel to choose an option:

1. You can discover more specific choices on the Share panel, which is accessed by selecting certain options.
2. Certain settings provide a window where you may share photos by logging in to an account. Screens allowing you to log in to your account and follow the instructions for preparing and posting photographs will appear when you want to share images with other services.

The Share panel in Windows' Organizer (left) and Photo Editor (right) are seen in the image below. The Photo Editor Share panel offers fewer choices. The Organizer's Share panel lacks a Burn Video DVD menu option, which is the only way the panels vary on a Mac.

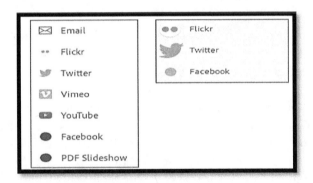

Facebook is available in both the Photo Editor Share and the Organizer panels, as you can see. A Facebook link has been restored to the Share options by Adobe. You will be sent to the new Elements Web function, which was released in 2023, if you choose Facebook from either option. Both devices have the same choices in the Share box. Compared to previous iterations, elements now offer fewer sharing possibilities. This is a result of some app developers ceasing to allow sharing from PC applications.

Sending pictures via email

It is not necessary to save your file in Elements, and then choose the image to attach to an email in your email software (such as Apple Mail or Outlook). Elements makes it simple to send pictures via email with a single click. **To send an image or artwork, follow these steps:**

↓ Choose the pictures you want to send to a friend in the Organizer.

- Choose Email Attachments from the Share menu. Elements launches the Organizer Preferences panel and prompts you to create an email account when you want to send photographs for the first time. If you have previously set up your email account, the Preferences tab will not appear. Click OK after entering your message in the fields.
- Click Next after selecting Convert Photos to JPEGs and selecting an attachment quality preset. Examine the file size shown in the Estimated Size box at the bottom of the screen after moving the Quality slider. Before emailing the image, you may need to adjust the file size in the Image Size box.
- Add recipients (optional). Options for inserting a message and adding recipients from an address book are available in the following panel. Adding individuals from your address book is not required. It's possible that the Select Recipients box has no recipients listed. In your email program's new message box, you may enter the recipients' email addresses. Depending on the email application you use, adding recipients on a Mac could require manual labor.
- Press the Next button. First, the picture or photos are resized to fit the output's dimensions. Elements will complete the sample shortly. After that, the images will be included in a fresh email message in your preferred email program. Elements adds the media to a fresh email message. You must switch to your email app in order to see the message and send the letter.
- Verify that the data in the To, Subject, and Attach fields is accurate. Next, press the Send button. By default, Elements will utilize your primary email client, which may or may not be your preferred email program. To access the Preferences box while in the Organizer, use Ctrl+K (or ⌘+K on a Mac). Then, to switch the default email program, select Email in the left pane. You may choose the email program you want Elements to use from a drop-down option in the Sharing settings. Elements may be utilized with web-based email applications. If you have a Yahoo!, Gmail, or other email account, you may send the photographs using your email application. If you choose "Other" in the Email Preferences, you will need to provide your SMTP server and port number. Ask your Internet Service Provider (ISP) for assistance if you need assistance configuring email for accounts that aren't listed in Email Preferences.

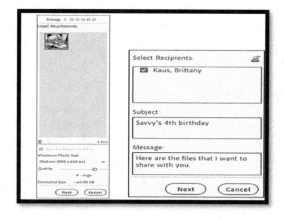

Interacting with Adobe Premiere Elements

Some of the features in the Share and create panels need Adobe Premiere Elements. Adobe Premiere Elements are required for burning videos, DVDs, Blu-rays, online video sharing, and mobile phones and players. You may try Adobe Premiere Elements for free for 30 days if any of this piques your curiosity. If you believe Premiere Elements is a helpful tool, you can get it from the Adobe Store. By selecting one of the video-sharing options in the Share panel, you may get a trial edition of Adobe Premiere Elements. After that, you'll be prompted to download Premiere Elements' trial edition.

Posting images on social media

You have several possibilities for making orders and sharing photographs on a variety of service networks. Since we can't cover all of Elements' services in this space, we'll only take Flickr, Facebook, and Twitter as examples of how to get in touch with a service provider. Examine your existing service selections to determine if there are any alternative services that may be of interest. Flickr and other services were concealed in the More Options drop-down menu in previous versions of Elements. Experienced users will now see that they are now accessible in the Share panel as buttons.

Using Twitter and Facebook to share pictures

You may connect to Twitter directly using Elements. Twitter may be selected in the Share box. Elements launches the web browser of your choice and takes you to the Twitter website. You must enter your login credentials to verify that you are the owner of this account. You may enter your tweet in Elements when your account has been validated. After that, add it to your account by clicking the Tweet icon.

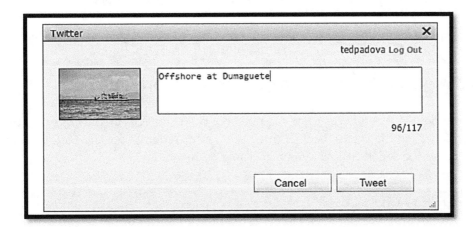

Posting images to Facebook using Elements is feasible, but it must be done using Elements Web.

Making use of additional online resources

If you know how to publish photographs to one service, you can easily follow the same procedures to post photos to any other service that Elements supports. A popup requesting you to verify your account is the first thing you see. For instance, whether using Twitter, Flickr, or Facebook. You may log in to the service and create a new account if you'd like to. Simply follow the instructions provided by each provider when you visit a website to share images, print photos, or create items like picture frames.

Generating Slideshows in PDF

The Share column has a PDF Slideshow option. Clicking this option after selecting photographs in the Organizer will bring up the Share panel with the same choices as when using email. The only difference between this option and sending your photographs is that the selected images are stored as a PDF and then sent to the recipients you choose in the Share box.

Commonly asked questions

Adobe Photoshop Elements 2025: To who is it intended?

Anyone who wishes to edit and create with their images can use Photoshop Elements 2025. It is offered as a three-year license with no ongoing subscription costs. It provides:
- Simple editing with automation and artificial intelligence
- Detailed instructions for editing and producing
- Fun methods for creating and sharing prints, effects, gifts, and creations
- An organizer that makes it simple to locate and classify your pictures
- Beta companion apps for mobile and web

Does Photoshop Elements require a subscription?

No, the license has a three-year term and is a one-time payment. It is not necessary to have a subscription.

In what ways does the three-year license operate?

There is no monthly or yearly recurring membership costs needed for the complete three-year license period. When the license expires three years after redemption, the Editor will no longer be available, but the Organizer will remain available permanently.

What distinguishes Premiere Elements from Photoshop Elements?

- Photoshop Elements is made for photographers who want quick and simple ways to edit their images, make them seem amazing, create unique designs, print them, and share them with friends and family.
- Premiere Elements is made for those who record videos and want to quickly and easily edit them to make them look fantastic, create entertaining projects, and create polished films that they can share with friends and family.
- For convenient access to all images and videos, both applications use the same organizer.
- They are available for purchase separately or in a bundle.

Is it possible to try Photoshop Elements for free?

Yes, a seven-day, fully functional trial of Photoshop Elements is available for free download. You can buy straight from the trial software after the trial time is over, saving you the trouble of downloading and installing it again.

Is it better to purchase Photoshop Elements 2025 or the Photoshop Elements & Premiere Elements 2025 bundle?

If you enjoy shooting and sharing images and videos, purchase the bundle to:
- To make all of your pictures and movies easily accessible, use the common organizer.
- Collaboratively edit and distribute images and movies.

What are the companion apps for the web and mobile beta?

For licensed customers of Photoshop Elements 2025 and Premiere Elements 2025, the Elements 2025 products feature companion apps for the web and mobile devices. The apps are accessible in English, French, German, and Japanese and are presently in beta testing. They come with two gigabytes of free cloud storage. You can enjoy your images and movies on the web, mobile apps, and Elements Organizer thanks to auto-syncing.
- **Web beta application**
  - View, access, and distribute images and movies.
  - You may alter the appearance of your images, add animated overlays, and change the background of your photos automatically.
  - Make picture collages, slideshows with images and videos, and share them on social media using QR codes.
- **Beta app for mobile**
  - View, access, and distribute images and movies.

- Utilize sliders to modify light, color, and effects; trim, straighten, and eliminate backgrounds with one-click Quick Actions; and add entertaining pattern overlays to images.
- View creations from Elements Web, do one-click picture edits, and import images from a variety of files and folders on your phone.

Beta apps for mobile and web

- Enjoy your images and movies from anywhere by having them automatically sync with the Elements Organizer, the web, and mobile apps.
- Store images and movies on the cloud for usage on mobile devices, desktop computers, and websites.
- To see images and videos on the web and mobile apps, upload them from your PC.
- Using an email or link, post images and videos from the app to the social media sites of your choice.

What distinguishes Photoshop Elements from Photoshop, Photoshop Lightroom Classic, and Lightroom subscription versions?

- Customers who are new to photo editing and want a simple way to organize, edit, create, and share their photographs are the target audience for Photoshop Elements. AI and automated alternatives produce excellent results that can be used as a springboard for creative research or enjoyed as is. Photoshop Elements is available for purchase as a three-year license; there are no ongoing subscription costs.
- The industry standard for producing eye-catching photos, graphics, and 3D artwork is Photoshop. It requires a subscription.
- Professional and experienced amateur photographers may import, process, organize, and display vast amounts of digital photos with Lightroom Classic, which meets their desktop workflow needs. It requires a subscription.
- The cloud-based program Lightroom makes it simple for users to edit, arrange, store, and share their images on desktop computers, mobile devices, and the internet. It requires a subscription.

What distinguishes Photoshop Express from Photoshop Elements?

- Both Photoshop Express and Photoshop Elements are capable of producing stunning images. Every product is designed to work with various photo editing scenarios. The equipment you have, the extent of your alterations, and your photographic style all play a role in choosing which photo editing program to employ.
- Customers that desire an easy way to organize, edit, produce, and share their photographs are the target audience for Photoshop Elements. AI and automated alternatives produce excellent results that can be used as a springboard for creative

research or enjoyed as is. Large, complicated files with many layers and a lot of data can be handled by it. You may make extensive changes and enhancements because it has a lot more tools and functionality than Photoshop Express. Photoshop Elements can radically change a photo, whereas Photoshop Express can only make it better. Photoshop Elements is available for purchase as a three-year license; there are no ongoing subscription costs.

- Photoshop Express is an iOS and Android mobile app that can be found in a number of app stores. It utilizes the camera roll on your mobile device. The app's editing features are designed to make quick adjustments on your phone, and it was created for smartphone photography. It's perfect for applying effects like text and light leaks as well as fast adjustments like overlays and filters. In addition to editing exposure, shadows, brightness, saturation, and other aspects, users can alter opacity and tone coloring.

I edit my photos with free software. For what reason should I think about Photoshop Elements 2025?

- The majority of free photo processors only provide a small selection of editing capabilities. Since it gives users of all skill levels what they need to organize, edit, create, and share, Photoshop Elements is the most popular consumer picture editing program. This includes:
- AI and automated tools that make it simple to edit, enhance, or transform any image into your artistic canvas
- Using Smart Tags, facial recognition, and other technologies, the organizer can quickly locate images and videos and clear out clutter.
- One-click fixes with Quick Edit
- To improve your skills, try these fifty-nine guided edits. Simply follow the instructions to make simple adjustments, creative creations, and everything in between. For full photo changes, try Advanced Edit.
- Enjoy your favorite images as gorgeous prints, gallery-quality wall art, or make one-of-a-kind keepsakes for loved ones (US only).
- The capacity to produce captivating photo reels, slideshows, collages, and motivational quote graphics for social network sharing
- Unique templates
- Access to companion apps on the web and mobile devices (beta)